PEACE

PEACE

50 years of protest
1958–2008

Barry Miles

COLLINS & BROWN

First published in the United Kingdom in 2008 by
Collins & Brown
10 Southcombe Street
London
W14 0RA

An imprint of Anova Books Company Ltd

Produced by Essential Works
www.essentialworks.co.uk

ISBN 978-1-84340-457-6

A CIP catalogue for this book is available from the
British Library.

10 9 8 7 6 5 4 3 2 1

Reproduction by Rival Colour, UK
Printed and bound by Craft Print International Ltd,
Singapore

This book can be ordered direct from the publisher.
Contact the marketing department, but try your
bookshop first.

www.anovabooks.com

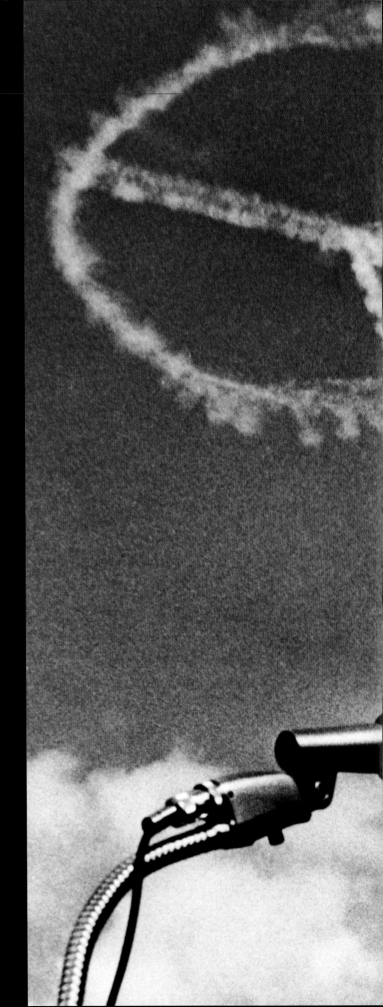

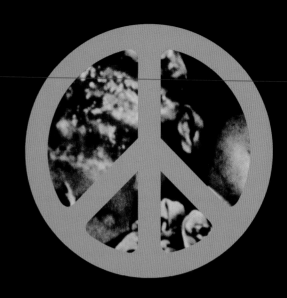

CONTENTS

Foreword

In August 1945, two American air force planes dropped atomic bombs on the Japanese cities of Hiroshima and Nagasaki. As a result of these attacks, hundreds of thousands of people died, many instantaneously, others soon after. But the tragic and devastating consequences did not end there: over the months and years that followed, tens of thousands more died from the impact of radiation. In all, around 340,000 people had been killed by those two bombs by 1950. Thus began the nuclear age.

As technology has advanced over the last hundred years, so too has humanity's ability to kill on a scale inconceivable to previous generations. From the millions killed in World War I to those dead in the gas chambers of the Nazi extermination camps; from those vaporised by the atomic bombs on Hiroshima and Nagasaki to those torn to pieces by cluster bombs or dying a slow death from uranium poisoning: every death is a cause of sorrow and suffering. That our beautiful world, with its bounteous resources and talented peoples, should be such a killing field, is incomprehensible to the majority of humanity.

Those of us who love life, and wish to live in peace with others, are undoubtedly the majority. And from this majority, across the world over the past decades, has sprung a movement for peace, which has sought to prevent war and end the threat of nuclear annihilation. In Britain in the post-World War II period, that desire for peace has primarily been articulated by the Campaign for Nuclear Disarmament, which arose out of public desire to prevent the world racing towards nuclear Armageddon. But other movements worldwide have shared the same goals and together we have worked to prevent that catastrophe and sought to end wars and bloodshed. Indeed, whatever organisation people may belong to, whatever country they may inhabit, those working for peace are fighting for humanity against the horror of war.

That cause has come to be symbolised by the peace sign, the history of which this book so beautifully records.

As CND celebrates its fiftieth anniversary in 2008, so too do we celebrate the anniversary of the peace sign. It was produced for the first Aldermaston march for nuclear disarmament in 1958 and became CND's own symbol. The artist, Gerald Holtom, explained the symbol in the following way: 'First the semaphore initials for 'N' and 'D'. Second, the broken cross meant the death of man, the circle the unborn child. It represented the threat of nuclear weapons to all mankind and, because this was new, the threat to the unborn child.' So Holtom sought, through this symbol, to express the danger of radiation poisoning to future life – a fear that was very sharp at that time, before the atmospheric testing of nuclear weapons had been banned.

But the power of Holtom's design rapidly transcended its origins as an antinuclear sign – and we in the antinuclear movement have been delighted that our symbol has come to be recognised universally as the sign for peace. Very soon after the first Aldermaston march, the symbol came to adorn badges, posters, leaflets, mugs, clothes, banners; and ever since it has been graffitied on to walls and virtually any available flat surface all over the world.

The peace sign stands for life and hope, it represents a vision of a better world – a world without war and the fear of nuclear annihilation. And for me, and countless others across the world, the sign stands for that vision becoming a reality.

Kate Hudson
Chair of the Campaign for Nuclear Disarmament

British graffiti artist Banksy created this banner for peace campaigner Brian Haw's Parliament Square protest against the invasion of Iraq by British and American forces. In 2007 it was hung in the Tate Britain museum as part of Mark Wallinger's exhibition, State Britain, which recreated Haw's demonstration in full.

INTRODUCTION

It took 200 years for the majority of Christians to decide upon the cross
as a symbol of their belief – an icon certainly easier to draw than a fish. There
have long been antiwar protests, but with the invention of weapons of mass
destruction, it took only 12 years for a new type of symbol to come into being:
the peace sign. To display the symbol set someone apart from the warmongers,
and although it began as a sign of opposition to nuclear weapons, over the
years it has come to represent the idea of peace itself. A renewed stand for
peace has never been more urgent. Current American military spending
equals that of the next 15 biggest nations combined, and in 2007 the UK signed
a $90 billion deal to supply Saudi Arabia with fighter aircraft. At a time when
the world desperately needs peace, 2008 marks 50 years for the peace sign.

The story of a symbol

It is the most commonly used symbol of protest in the world. Instantly recognisable in Europe, the Americas, Africa, Asia, Australasia and both Poles as the universal sign for peace, the peace symbol became 50 years old in 2008. This book tells the story of the growing power of a sign specifically designed for just one protest march, organised by a small group of British antiwar activists – The Direct Action Committee Against Nuclear War – who wanted to stop the manufacture and testing of nuclear weapons in Britain.

The Direct Action Committee originally envisioned a few dozen protesters walking from London to Aldermaston, the British government's secret nuclear weapons factory, where they hoped to talk with the people employed there to persuade them to stop making weapons of mass destruction. The march was planned for the Easter weekend in 1958, but just as the organisers began making arrangements there was a major development in the British peace movement.

On 28 January, most of the disparate peace groups in Britain decided to join forces to create one large mass movement that was to be called the Campaign for Nuclear Disarmament. This movement was launched at a public meeting in London on 17 February 1958.

The meeting was well attended. Its organising committee included famous writers, historians, philosophers, politicians and clergy, and they had used the press and broadcasting media to assemble several thousand like-minded, mostly middle-class British people. The public response was gratifying: banning nuclear weapons became the debate of the day, occupying hundreds of column inches in the newspapers and the subject of numerous radio and television discussion programmes. The Direct Action Committee suddenly found that hundreds, if not thousands, of people wanted to attend their protest march. It went down in history as the first

Aldermaston march, and although not actually organised by the newly formed CND, it was, in effect, the first CND demonstration.

The Direct Action Committee had asked one of its members, graphic artist Gerald Holtom, to design banners and badges for the march so that the public would know what they were protesting about. After considerable thought, he chose the semaphore symbols for 'N' and 'D' to stand for 'nuclear disarmament' and enclosed them within a circle – the symbol of life. Badges were soon made, huge banners silk-screened, lollipop-style hand signs constructed, and the CND symbol, later known as the peace symbol, had its first public outing on that Easter march to Aldermaston.

It wasn't the first public protest against the superpowers' use of nuclear weapons as a 'deterrent' against another world war, but it was by far the most important – not only because it had a coherent and easily understood central message of protest, but most importantly, because it had a new, instantly identifiable logo.

Original and striking, Holtom's monochrome design quickly became an internationally adopted symbol of opposition to nuclear weapons. After seeing this eye-catching flag being carried through the streets of London, reproduced in newspaper photographs, and on television and cinema newsreels of the Easter 1958 Aldermaston march, people around the

In the 1950s, the mushroom cloud became a potent image of atomic weapons and their fearsome power just as the peace sign became a symbol of the growing opposition to their use.

world started painting, sewing, and spraying the CND logo onto their own clothes and banners. Before long, antinuclear protesters from Aldermaston, England to Alaska, USA, and from Adelaide, Australia to Akita, Japan, were marching to protest for nuclear disarmament, united beneath the CND symbol.

Since then, the CND sign has been appropriated by scores of different protest movements. In Greece in 1963, for example, the Committee of 100 used it to protest against American nuclear bases, and then as a rallying flag after the government murdered the leader of the Greek antinuclear movement – the independent member of parliament, Gregory Lambrakis.

It was the hippies of the late 1960s who first drafted the logo to represent 'peace' rather than just nuclear disarmament; a use adopted by unwilling American GIs drafted to fight in Vietnam. Not long after this, feminists joined it to the symbol for female (a circle with a + at the bottom) and carried it on women's rights marches across the globe.

Today it can be found on T-shirts and hugely expensive items of clothing, and sprayed on the walls of slums and shanty towns in Latin America and Africa. It can also be seen on banners and badges of the third and fourth generation of international antinuclear protesters around the world. By 2008, just as it was 50 years earlier, the CND logo (which has never been copyrighted by the organisation, a decision that has undoubtedly encouraged its widespread use) was in use at antinuclear and antiwar protests the world over.

This book begins with the destruction of Hiroshima and Nagasaki by thermonuclear bombs to show the reasons why the atomic bomb, as opposed to conventional weapons, caused such fear and paranoia in the world. It describes the background to the invention of the bomb and how Russia, Britain, and France quickly moved to develop bombs of their own. A simultaneous growth of antiatomic

bomb sentiment also grew around the world, particularly in Japan, which had not only suffered from having its civilian population exposed to nuclear attack, but had its basic food supplies disrupted when its fishing boats were engulfed in clouds of radioactive dust 190 km (118 miles) from an American test explosion, eight years later.

This book examines the growth of British and American peace groups, and tells the story of the peace sign's actual creation. Gerald Holtom not only designed the symbol for the movement, but also did drawings to show his design in use. He envisaged the complete scenario, banners, pennants and handheld 'lollipop' signs.

It was an extraordinary exercise in 'branding', when that concept was still in its infancy. All-too-familiar commercial trademarks promote million-dollar advertising campaigns, but noncommercial logos that have entered the popular consciousness since the 19th century, are few and far between: the communist hammer-and-sickle, the red cross, the swastika and the peace sign.

Many people have commercialised the image on T-shirts, on hats, badges and wristbands, but no matter how it is used, in what garish colours or inappropriate a context, it always means the same thing: peace.

One of Gerald Holtom's original sketches of the peace-sign design.

'There is no flag large enough to cover the shame of killing innocent people.'

– HOWARD ZINN

An aerial view taken half a year after the atomic bomb wreaked total devastation on the city of Hiroshima.

'I AM BECOME DEATH'

This devastating quote, loosely translated from the Sanskrit *Bhagavad Gita*, may have entered the mind of nuclear scientist Robert Oppenheimer, a Sanskrit scholar, when the first atomic bomb tests were made. There is no question that many of the brilliant minds who helped develop nuclear weapons in the USA to forestall their use by the Germans in World War II had serious reservations about unleashing them on Japan. General Dwight D. Eisenhower, American commander of European operations, opposed their use. But President Harry S. Truman believed that the bombs would save lives by shortening the conflict with Japan. His chief foreign policy adviser, James F. Byrnes, hoped the bombs would also deter the Russians from moving into Asia, as they had into Europe.

Doomsday: 6 August 1945

At its peak, the wartime population of Hiroshima was 380,000 people, but by the summer of 1945, it had been reduced to 240,000 by several evacuation programmes. Almost every night for weeks, there had been air-raid warnings, sometimes several in one night because American B-29s used Lake Biwa, to the northeast of Hiroshima, as a rendezvous point regardless of which Japanese city they intended to bomb. But the planes never came. The fact that Hiroshima had been spared by the Superfortresses had made the population very anxious; it was as if the Americans were saving the city for something special.

At Tinian Island in the West Pacific's Marianas chain, a specially modified B-29 Superfortress was being prepared for a special mission at the North Field airbase. The aircraft commander was Col. Paul Tibbets, commander of the 509th Composite Group, created specifically to develop and employ the atomic bomb. Tibbets had previously been squadron commander of the 340th Bomb Squadron, 97th Bombardment Group based in England. He had flown 25 missions over occupied Europe, including the first US B-17 Flying Fortress raid. In November 1942 he was transferred to Algeria where he led the bombing missions in support of the North African invasion. The following March, he was recalled to the USA, where he was involved with testing the new B-29 Superfortress. He flew about 400 hours of tests, making him the most experienced B-29 pilot at that time, with a tremendous knowledge of its range, limitations, and capabilities.

In September 1944, he was briefed on the top-secret Manhattan Project and given the job of organising and training a unit to deliver the new secret bombs. He was in charge of modifying a B-29 to do the job, and spent months in Los Alamos with flight test aeroplanes, testing ballistics and various detonators: The bombs were to explode in the air, not on impact, so Tibbets and his crew would need to have time

to get safely out of range. He called the delivery aircraft the *Enola Gay*, his mother's name.

On 5 August, an atomic bomb, code-named Little Boy and weighing almost 5 tons, was loaded into the front bomb bay of the modified B-29 Superfortress. It was 3 m (10 ft) long and about 75 cm (30 in) across, and estimated to have an explosive force of 20,000 tons of TNT. Early next morning, two B-29s took off from North Field at Tinian Island base as weather scouts, followed an hour later at 2:45 A.M. by *Enola Gay*.

TARGET HIROSHIMA

Enola Gay began its flight with a 10-man crew, followed by two observation planes that were carrying cameras and scientific equipment. Just after 6:00 A.M. Navy Capt. Deak Parsons and Lt. Morris Jeppson climbed down to the bomb bay to arm and complete the assembly of the bomb; they had not wanted the bomb to be fully armed immediately, because several heavily loaded B-29s had crashed on takeoff, and they were concerned that Little Boy might destroy half the island. At about 7:00 A.M. Japanese radar detected the aircraft and broadcast an air-raid alert to the Hiroshima area, but because the people were used to false alarms, most of them chose to ignore it. An hour later another air-raid warning was broadcast over the radio when two B-29s were detected heading toward Hiroshima.

Col. P. W. Tibbets, standing in front of the Boeing B-29 Superfortress, which was used to drop the atomic bomb on the Japanese city of Hiroshima.

Once again, people ignored it. At 8:14 A.M., the *Enola Gay* was cruising at 26,000 ft (7,924 m) above Hiroshima, too high for any anti-aircraft guns. Commander Paul Tibbets released the bomb. It was designed to explode at an altitude of 1,900 ft (580 m), where it would have the largest destructive effect. It took 57 seconds to reach detonation height at 08:14 and 20 seconds, Hiroshima time.

On 6 August 1945, it was a still day and already hot when people went to work that morning. Those who survived the blast did not recall any noise, they heard no roar, just saw a blinding flash of white light, which seemed to move from east to west toward the surrounding hills; however, 20 miles away, fishermen heard a tremendous explosion. A huge column of fire and smoke rose in the air, sucking air in beneath it, causing a firestorm. The mushroom-shaped cloud billowed upward, eventually reaching a height of 45,000 ft (13,715 m). The crew of the *Enola Gay* could see it as a distant pillar of smoke and ash, towering way above them.

'My God, what have we done?', copilot Capt. Robert Lewis wrote in the plane's log book. The *Enola Gay* landed at Tinian airbase at 2:58 P.M. to be greeted by a jubilant General Spaatz and a large contingent of top brass. Col Tibbets was awarded the Distinguished Service Cross, and the rest of the crew received air medals.

ANNIHILATION

The centre of the blast was later determined to be just a few yards southeast of the Shima Hospital in the city centre. This was calculated by triangulating the shadows caused by the flash of the bomb, which had sheared off the surface of granite and darkened concrete to a reddish tint, leaving prints of anything blocking the light. Some of these appeared distinct: the handle of a gas pump had been projected onto a wall 2,404 m (2,630 yd) from the blast, while the outline of towers of buildings were superimposed on other buildings far away.

The Hiroshima Chamber of Industry and Commerce was the only building near the centre of the bomb blast that was left standing. It has been kept that way as a reminder of the tragedy.

Most sinister were the shadows of human beings whose actual bodies were vaporised, leaving silhouettes: a house painter was burned into the side of a building in the act of dipping his brush in the paint can; someone in a horse and cart on the bridge near the Museum of Science and Industry was caught in the act of whipping the horse, his image was etched into the pavement. The temperature on the ground at the centre of the blast was estimated to have been 6,000 °C (10,832 °F): enough to melt the mica in the granite of the gravestones in a cemetery over 347 m (380 yd) away, and dissolve the type of grey tiles used in Hiroshima whose melting point was 1,500 °C (2,732 °F). Nothing could survive, and little did; the casualties were appalling. The blast killed 95 per cent of the people within a half mile of the centre and many thousands farther away.

COUNTING THE DEAD

Almost 100,000 people perished or were doomed to die within days of burns or severe radiation poisoning; a further 100,000 were injured either by the blast, falling buildings, or by the fires that broke out, started by broken electrical cables or the hot coals of smashed kitchen stoves. In one school, with 620 children, only two survived the blast, and one of them died a week later from radiation poisoning.

The initial figures showed 78,150 people dead, 13,983 missing, and 37,425 badly injured, but as the ruins were cleared, many hundreds more bodies were found in the rubble. The symptoms of radiation sickness had not yet begun to appear. It is now estimated that the total number of people killed in Hiroshima from the blast, from injuries, and from radiation poisoning by the end of 1945 was close to 140,000. Hundreds died of radiation poisoning in subsequent years.

The casualty figures might not have been so horrendous had medical help been available, but large numbers of people died because the medical staff was incapacitated and medical equipment destroyed. There were 150 doctors

The Allied fire bombing of German cities, though not on the nuclear scale of Hiroshima and Nagasaki, had a devastating effect, as did the German incendiary attacks on Coventry, the 'blitz' on London, and the bombing of other UK centres. Here, survivors cook on a makeshift stove in the ruins of Nuremberg.

'An eye for an eye only ends up making the whole world blind.'

– MAHATMA GANDHI

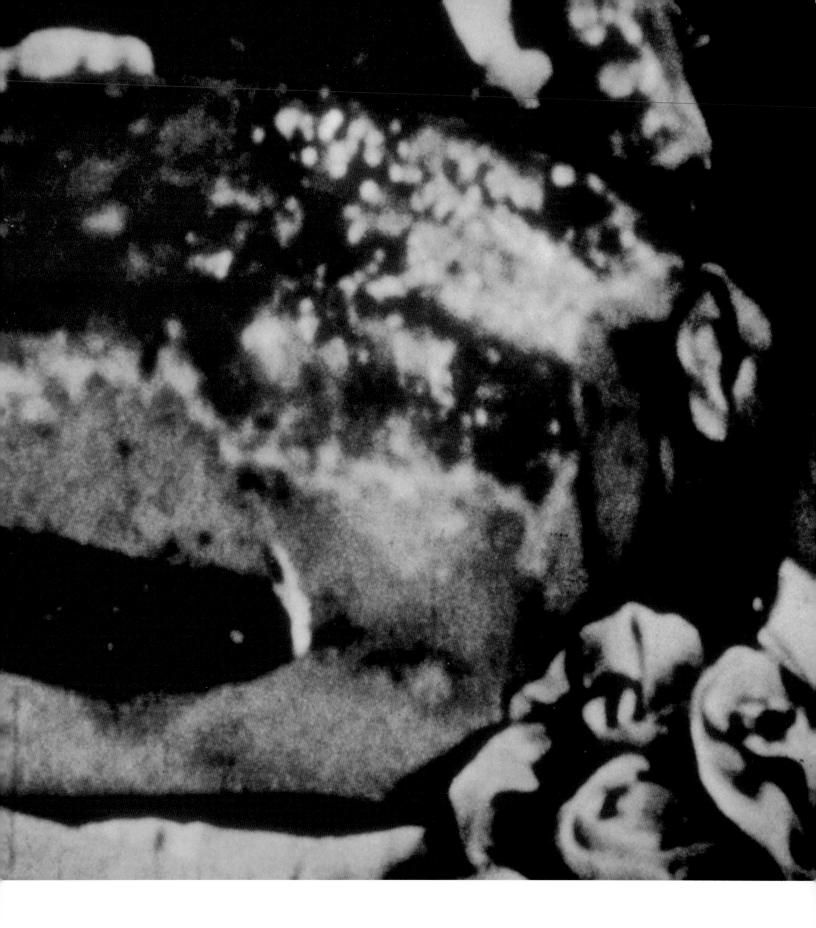

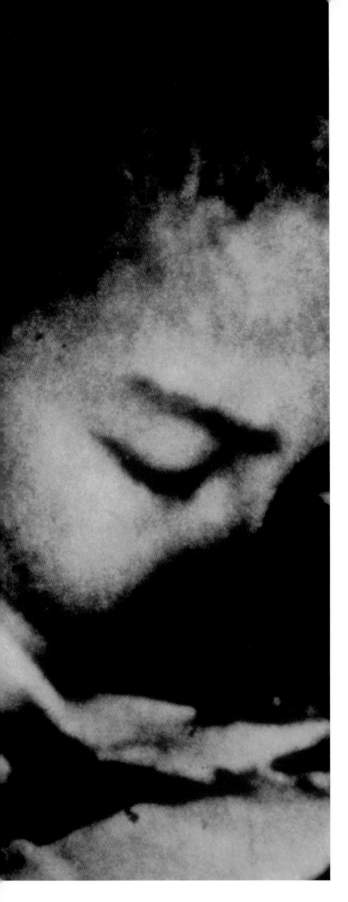

There were some survivors. This young boy, Sumiteru Taniguchi, was severely burned by the A-bomb blast at Nagasaki but later recovered and lived to an old age.

in Hiroshima on 5 August, but 65 were killed immediately and most of the others were injured, some of them badly. There were 1,780 nurses in the city, but after the blast 1,654 were either dead or too severely injured to perform their duties. In the Red Cross hospital just 6 doctors out of the 30 on staff were actually able to care for people – only one doctor was uninjured – and of the hospital's more than 200 nurses, only 10 were capable of functioning. Because the Red Cross hospital was Hiroshima's biggest, more than 10,000 injured people made their way across the broken city in the hope of being treated there.

... AND THE DYING

The hospital was swamped. Its 600 beds were already full before the bomb went off, with people injured by the US bombing of factories near Hiroshima. Patients lay in the corridors, in the hallways, on the steps and in the driveway, but more and more arrived, supporting each other, sometimes in family groups, some naked or wearing burned clothing, some vomiting as they walked, many terribly burned, skin hanging in great folds from their faces and arms.

   The blast had made patterns on some people, where suspenders and straps and buckles had shielded skin from the heat. As white cloth reflected the heat and dark colours absorbed it, on some women the flower pattern of their kimonos had been burned into their flesh. The injured lay in the streets for blocks around, moaning, vomiting, and dying as the skeleton staff frantically bandaged the cuts and abrasions, disregarding those who were only lightly injured; the most the doctors could do was prevent people from bleeding to death. All around, people died as they waited to be seen.

   That day, people had been clearing fire lanes, and many of those killed and injured were schoolgirls who had left their classrooms that morning to help with the fire prevention. They waited silently, in pain, along with the others.

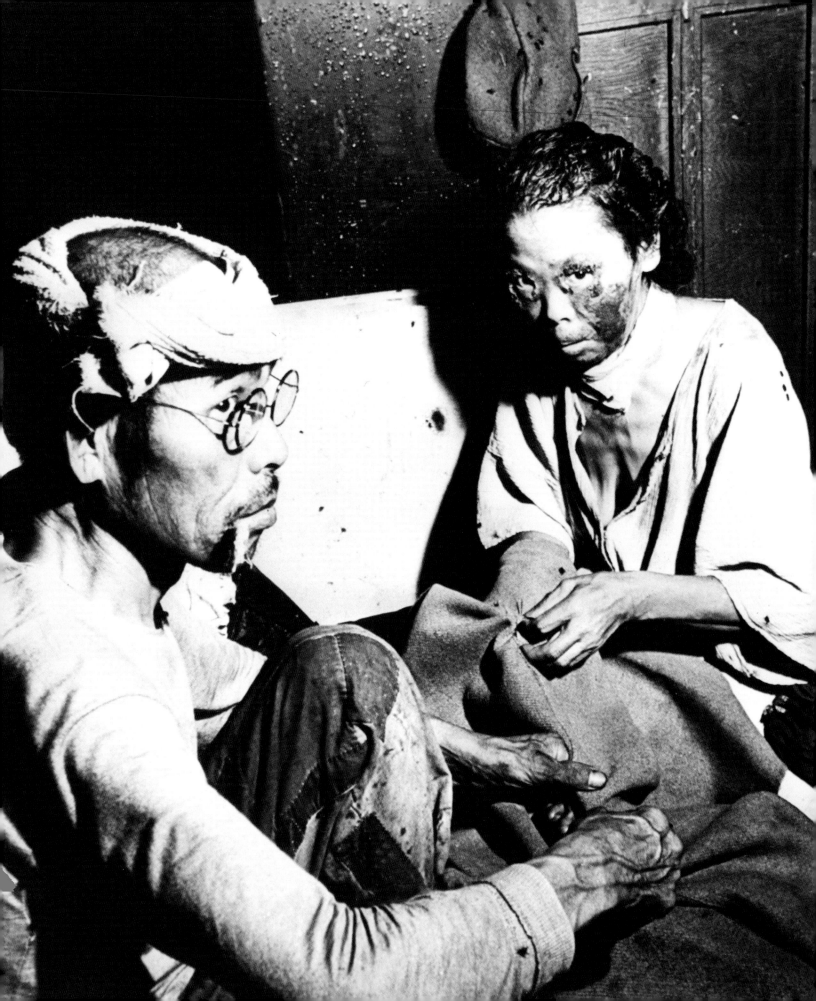

BLACK RAIN

About 45 mintues after the blast, a black rain began to descend on Hiroshima, falling heavily for about an hour in most places, mainly in the area to the northwest of the city. It stuck to the windows, leaving long, sinister black trails. Filled with black soot from vaporised buildings, it was oily and sticky and contained high levels of radioactivity, contaminating areas some distance from the hypocentre. Many people exposed to the rain, away from the centre, developed radiation sickness and died. Fish died in ponds and rivers, and people who drank water from wells suffered from diarrhoea for three months.

Although Japan exercised strict building regulations, introduced after the 1923 earthquake, little of the city was left standing, and of the city's 90,000 buildings, 62,000 were destroyed and 6,000 so badly damaged that they were beyond repair. In the city centre only five buildings were usable without major repairs.

The blast wave shattered windows 12 miles away in the suburbs. At the hypocentre of the explosion (ground zero directly below the explosion), the blast was more downward than from the side, which is why the Prefectural Industrial Promotional Hall – housing the Chamber of Industry and Commerce and now known as the *Genbaku*, or A-Bomb Dome – survived. It was only 150 m (165 yd) from the centre, but the dome seems to have deflected much of the force away from the structural elements, even though the roof was vaporized. Built by the Czech architect Jan Letzel, the ruin was designated as the Hiroshima Peace Memorial. In 1996, it was made a World Heritage Site by the UN Educational, Scientific, and Cultural Organisation (UNESCO) over the objections of the United States and China.

NAGASAKI

On August 9, three days after the destruction of Hiroshima, an atom bomb called Fat Man was dropped on the city of Nagasaki. The timing of

the second attack was delegated to Col. Tibbets, pilot of the *Enola Gay*, in his capacity as commander of the 509th Composite Group. A five-day period of bad weather was predicted from 10 August onwards, so the original date for the raid of 11 August was moved forwards. The primary target was the city of Kokura, but when commander Major Charles Sweeney arrived over the city in the B-29 Superfortress *Bockscar*, it was seven-tenths covered by cloud.

Sweeney's orders required a visual attack, and after three runs over Kokura, he turned to his secondary target, the port of Nagasaki. At 11:01 A.M. there was a last-minute break in cloud cover over Nagasaki, giving Sweeney's crew the visual target they needed. In fact, bombardier Capt. Kermit Beahan missed the planned target by nearly 3 km (2 miles). Fat Man exploded at 469 m (1,540 feet) above the city's industrial zone, northwest of the planned hypocentre, halfway between the Mitsubishi Steel and Arms Works in the south and the Mitsubishi-Urakami Ordnance Works to the north, where torpedoes were made.

DEVASTATION

This resulted in much of the city being protected by a range of hills, but the casualties were still devastating. There were an estimated 240,000 residents in Nagasaki at the time of the bombing. Of these, about 70,000 were killed instantly by the blast and collapsing buildings, and about 60,000 were injured. A further 10,000 are thought to have died in the following weeks and months from radiation poisoning and the results of injury and burns.

Recent statistics, which include people who died years later of radiation sickness and long-term related illnesses, put the total Japanese civilians killed by the bombs on Hiroshima and Nagasaki at 360,000. (The number of Japanese civilians killed by bombing in World War II was 580,000. Japanese military deaths were 2,041,000. The USA lost 407,000 military personnel, some dying in Japanese POW camps near Hiroshima

Two days after the Hiroshima bomb blast, injured casualities were being treated in a makeshift clinic in a bank building.

Two survivors in
the shattered city
of Hiroshima are
photographed by
American naval
personnel in November
1945, three months after
the bombing.

'Either war is obsolete
or men are.'

– R. BUCKMINSTER FULLER

and Nagasaki, and 11,200 civilians, mostly in the Merchant Marine. Britain had 382,600 military killed and 67,800 civilians.)

LINGERING DEATH

Anyone within 3 km (2 miles) of the hypocentre, particularly those within 900 m (980 yd) of it, received life-threatening doses of radiation, many of them dying within a few days. Radiation seriously damages the liver, the cells that line the digestive tract, nerve cells, and other internal organs. It destroys the bone marrow's ability to produce red blood corpuscles and reduces the production of blood platelets, which aid blood clotting. It kills white blood cells, the body's main defence against illness, and also causes fever and diarrhoea, leaving people vulnerable to infection.

With a dose of 800 rems (the measure of radiation dosage) or more, death occurs between 2 and 14 days. Half of the people exposed to 450 rems will die, and survivors can expect an early death from cancer, particularly leukemia, cancer of the blood.

An unusual number of hibakusha – those exposed to radiation in Hiroshima and Nagasaki – began to develop leukemia in the 1950s, followed by cancers with longer latency periods: thyroid cancer, lung cancer, breast cancer, cancers of the stomach, the reproductive organs, and the urinary tract. Children grew up stunted and deformed. And in the late 1960s some survivors began to show chromosome aberrations, leading to fears of mutation, sickness, and deformity in future generations.

About two weeks after the blast, wounds that had appeared to be healing began to swell and become inflamed. People's hair fell out and they had headaches and diarrhoea. After a month gums bled, fevers developed, and their white blood cell count dropped sharply. Many succumbed to infection and died. In the following two or three years, it was found that people's burns were healing with strange, thick pink rubberlike scar tissue, as if some alien creature had attached itself to them. These were keloid tumours, and they developed mostly in teenagers. They were itchy and ugly, and Japanese doctors tried at first to operate, but it was later found that it was best to leave them alone because in time they shrank naturally and could be more easily removed. In the late 1940s, photographs of these terrible scars helped inform public opinion about the terrible consequences of nuclear warfare.

EARLY WARNING

An early intimation of such horrors was at a physics conference held in Washington, DC, in January 1939, which discussed the technical problems of making an atom bomb, based on the nuclear fission of uranium. Many argued that the amount of uranium required would be too great to make the it work, while others thought a few pounds would suffice. All agreed that such a bomb would have awesome power.

Scientists in various countries were already conducting research in this area, including Nazi Germany, and on 2 August 1939, three Jewish scientists who had fled to the USA to escape persecution in Europe – Albert Einstein, Leo Szilard, and Eugene Wigner – wrote to President Roosevelt expressing concern that the Nazis were hoping to develop a nuclear bomb.

The text was mostly by Szilard, but Einstein was already well known and highly respected, and a letter from him would certainly carry more weight. They warned that discoveries made within the last four months by Enrico Fermi and Leo Szilard in the USA and by Frédéric Joliot-Curie in France showed that, in the near future, it would be possible to set up a nuclear chain reaction in a large mass of uranium. They warned that this phenomenon could be used in the construction of bombs and it was conceivable that a bomb of immense power could be manufactured. They gave the example of one such bomb being carried into a port, which would likely destroy not only the whole port but some of the surrounding territory as well.

Pioneers of the nuclear age: atomic theorist Albert Einstein and the founding father of American theoretical physics, Robert Oppenheimer.

Roosevelt's response was to form the Advisory Committee on Uranium, which first met on 21 October 1939. A mere $6,000 was budgeted for uranium experiments. It was not until 6 December 1941, that the American government accelerated the research into nuclear weapons.

THE MANHATTAN PROJECT

In the summer of 1942, the Army Corps of Engineers created the separate Manhattan Engineering District – named after their initial location – under the command of Brigadier Gen. Leslie Groves. On 15 October, Groves appointed New Yorker, Robert Oppenheimer, as the scientific director of a secret government laboratory devoted to the invention of an atomic bomb. Harvard graduate, Oppenheimer, had done his postgraduate studies at the famous Cavendish Laboratory in Cambridge, England,

directed by Ernest Rutherford, and had moved from there in 1926 to study under Max Born at the University of Göttingen, where he received his Ph.D. the following year at the age of only 22. The professor who took his oral examination said afterwards, 'Phew, I'm glad that's over. He was on the point of questioning me.'

Back in the USA, he quickly made a name for himself, becoming known as the founding father of American theoretical physics. He was a difficult, brilliant man, widely educated in areas well beyond scientific inquiry, who was the obvious choice to head a team of theoretical physicists in the development of a nuclear bomb.

On the afternoon of 2 December 1942, in a disused squash court under the west stands of Stagg Field Stadium at the University of Chicago, the Italian scientist Enrico Fermi and his team of scientists gazed anxiously at an enormous square

The first publicly released photograph of the type of nuclear weapon resembling Little Boy – the A-bomb that was dropped on Hiroshima.

balloon of rubberized cloth. Contained within this 7.92-m (26-ft)-high construction were over 6 tons of pure uranium, along with 34 tons of uranium oxide built into 400 tons of graphite blocks. This was an atomic pile, or primitive nuclear reactor. They had assembled it in the middle of a city of over three million people, in an operation that the Atomic Energy Commission later described as 'a possibly catastrophic experiment in one of the most densely populated areas of the nation'.

Fermi had received the Nobel Prize in 1938 for 'his discovery of new radioactive elements produced by neutron irradiation, and for the discovery of nuclear reactions brought about by slow neutrons' – in other words, for his work on nuclear fission. Einstein's mass-energy equation, $E=mc^2$, showed that enormous quantities of energy would be released by the conversion of mass into energy, and American scientists had convinced President Roosevelt that Fermi, who had managed to leave Italy before war broke out and was now living in the USA, should head a secret research team to split the atom.

The only things preventing a fission chain reaction from growing inside his atomic pile and destroying Chicago were a series of cadmium rods inserted into the side of the pile to absorb the free neutrons emitted by the radioactive uranium. As the long, slender rods were slowly inched out by George Weil, the only scientist actually working next to the reactor, the pile moved closer and closer to a self-sustaining fission chain reaction. At 3:25 P.M., Weil pulled out the last cadmium rod; Fermi checked his dials, and completed one final calculation on his ivory slide rule as his face broke into a smile.

'The reaction is self-sustaining', he told the assembled scientists. There was a ripple of applause from the rest of his team, who were watching from the old squash-court balcony. The reactor was generating about half a watt of electricity, just enough to power a small lightbulb, but it was proof that humans had finally unleashed and controlled the terrible power of the atom.

A bottle of Chianti and paper cups were passed around for everyone to drink a toast. The scientists then signed the bottle. Meanwhile, a coded message was sent to James Conant, one of the leaders of the Manhattan Project, reading: 'The Italian navigator has landed in the new world ... The natives were very friendly.' Fermi was transferred to Los Alamos as a general

'Peace cannot be kept by force. It can only be achieved by understanding.'

– ALBERT EINSTEIN

WORLD'S FIRST PROTEST AGAINST THE A-BOMB

Excerpts from the letter sent to President Truman that was drafted by Leo Szilard and signed by 68 members of the Metallurgical Laboratory in Chicago

A PETITION TO THE PRESIDENT OF THE UNITED STATES, July 17, 1945

... We, the undersigned scientists, have been working in the field of atomic power. Until recently, we have had to fear that the United States might be attacked by atomic bombs during this war and that her only defense might lie in a counterattack by the same means. Today, with the defeat of Germany, this danger is averted and we feel impelled to say what follows:

The war has to be brought speedily to a successful conclusion and attacks by atomic bombs may very well be an effective method of warfare. We feel, however, that such attacks on Japan could not be justified, at least not until the terms which will be imposed after the war on Japan were made public in detail and Japan were given an opportunity to surrender ...

The development of atomic power will provide the nations with new means of destruction. The atomic bombs at our disposal represent only the first step in this direction, and there is almost no limit to the destructive power which will become available in the course of their future development. Thus a nation which sets the precedent of using these newly liberated forces of nature for purposes of destruction may have to bear the responsibility of opening the door to an era of devastation on an unimaginable scale.

If after the war a situation is allowed to develop in the world which permits rival powers to be in uncontrolled possession of these new means of destruction, the cities of the United States as well as the cities of other nations will be continuous danger of sudden annihilation. All the resources of the United States, moral and material, may have to be mobilized to prevent the advent of such a world situation. Its prevention is at present the solemn responsibility of the United States—singled out by virtue of her lead in the field of atomic power ...

In view of the foregoing, we, the undersigned, respectfully petition: first, that you exercise your power as Commander-in-Chief to rule that the United States shall not resort to the use of atomic bombs in this war unless the terms which will be imposed upon Japan have been made public in detail and Japan knowing these terms has refused to surrender; second, that in such an event the question whether or not to use atomic bombs be decided by you in the light of the consideration presented in this petition as well as all the other moral responsibilities which are involved.

consultant, and in May 1944 he tested the world's third nuclear reactor, LOPO, the first to be fuelled by enriched uranium.

A BLACK DAY

One of the scientists in Chicago that historic day in 1942 was Leo Szilard, who later wrote that he had waited on the observation balcony until most people had left. He then turned to Fermi, shook his hand, and said: 'This will go down as a black day in the history of mankind.'

Enormous amounts of money were poured into the Manhattan Project, and after setbacks, one of which killed two scientists and badly injured another, it came time to test the device.

LOS ALAMOS

Oppenheimer's choice of Los Alamos as a location was determined by the fact he had a ranch nearby and knew the country. A short distance away was a private boys school called the Los Alamos Ranch School, which occupied 900 acres of mesa and ravine. The school buildings were at the top of a 2,286-m (7,500-ft) mesa named Parajarito or 'little bird', and the name Los Alamos – the Spanish name for the cottonwood – came from the trees that grew all around. The ranch was suitably isolated; Los Alamos is about 64 km (40 miles) north of Santa Fe and was bought by the government on 1 December 1942, using eminent domain.

Old boys of the school included the writer Gore Vidal and author William S. Burroughs, who later wrote: 'It was no accident that I went to the Los Alamos Ranch School where they couldn't wait to make the atom bomb and drop it on the Yellow Peril.' In February 1943 the bulldozers moved in and Oppenheimer and his team started building the laboratory. Meanwhile, significant work had been done on the development of nuclear fission itself.

On 16 July 1945, the world's first atomic bomb was tested at the Alamogordo Bombing Range, now called the White Sands Missile Range, at a site 56 km (35 miles) southeast of Socorro, New Mexico. It was code-named Trinity, a name Oppenheimer took from John Donne.

When asked if he chose it as a code word because it was innocuous sounding and could apply to many rivers and peaks in the southwest USA, he said: 'I did suggest it, but not on (that) ground ... Why I chose the name is not clear, but I know what thoughts were in my mind. There is a poem of John Donne's, written just before his death, which I know and love. From it a quotation: "As West and East / In all flatt Maps – and I am one – are on, / So death doth touch the Resurrection." *(Hymn to God My God, in My Sicknesses)*. That still does not make a Trinity, but in another, better-known devotional poem Donne opens, "Batter my heart, three person'd God" (*Holy Sonnets XIV*). Beyond this, I have no clues whatever.'

A THOUSAND SUNS

Instruments and cameras were arranged, and on 7 May a pretest explosion of 108 tons of TNT was exploded to calibrate the instruments. Since then, all nuclear explosions have been measured in their equivalent in tons of TNT. In order to generate the least amount of nuclear fallout and to get a better idea of how the bomb would behave when exploded above the ground and dropped from an aeroplane, the device – always referred to as 'the gadget' – was mounted at the top of a 20-m (65½-ft) steel tower. A number of bunkers were built to observe the test.

Robert Oppenheimer, General Thomas Farrell, and most of the top-level brass and scientists watched the test from one located only 16 km (10 miles) from the explosion, but General Groves, other scientists, and top brass were in a bunker situated 27 km (17 miles) away. More observers were in bunkers 32 km (20 miles) away. The device exploded at 05:29 and 45 seconds local time, and had an energy equivalent of 20,000 tons (20 kilotons) of TNT. The shock wave was felt over a distance of 160 km (100 miles), and the

'Never think that war, no matter how necessary, nor how justified, is not a crime.'

– ERNEST HEMINGWAY

mushroom cloud reached a height of 12 km (7½ miles). It rattled windows more than 322 km (200 miles) away. The surrounding mountains were illuminated brighter than daylight for two or three seconds. Oppenheimer said later that he recalled a verse from the *Bhagavad Gita*: 'If the radiance of a thousand suns were to burst at once into the sky, that would be like the splendour of the mighty one.' Some years later he recalled that another verse from the same holy book had entered his head: 'Now I am become Death, the destroyer of all.'

Oppeneheimer's brother, who was with him when the bomb went off, claims he simply said: 'It worked!'. The bomb melted the desert sand, leaving a crater of radioactive glass 3 m (10 ft) deep and 330 m (1,100 ft) in diameter. The supporting tower was completely vaporised. 'The lighting effects beggared description', noted an almost poetic report by General Farrell. 'The whole country was lighted by a searing light with the intensity many times that of the midday sun. It was golden, purple, violet, grey, and blue. It lighted every peak, crevasse, and ridge of the nearby mountain range with a clarity and beauty that cannot be described but must be seen to be imagined ... '. We had entered the nuclear age.

PETITION

Despite misgivings, Szilard had helped encourage Roosevelt to develop an atom bomb, knowing the Nazis were working on the same technology. In fact, he was probably a major voice in trying to convince the president to fund development in the first place. But in 1945 he would be among many scientists opposed to its use on civilian targets. At the beginning of World War II, bombing civilians was regarded as barbaric, but as the war progressed and people became accustomed to atrocities, attitudes changed. The Germans used fire bombs on UK cities, and the British destroyed Hamburg and Dresden by firestorm. The USA began using incendiaries on Tokyo and other Japanese cities, and its military talked of destroying them with atomic bombs.

Szilard and many of his fellow scientists signed a secret petition that was handed to President Truman, urging the government to demonstrate the bomb to the Japanese before using it on a civilian target; the Japanese were about to surrender but had yet to agree to terms. The sticking point involved the status of the Japanese emperor, but the USA wanted an unconditional surrender. Szilard and his colleagues were convinced that the Japanese would end the war

An aerial view of the atomic bomb testing site near Alamogordo, New Mexico, shows the huge crater created by the blast.

on American terms once they saw the power of the atom bomb. But the military argued that since they had only two bombs, they couldn't risk one not exploding as planned, even though more could have been built in about five weeks.

There was, in fact, considerable debate within military circles. General Eisenhower, supreme allied commander (and later president), told Truman that he was opposed to using the atomic bomb on Japanese cities. 'I voiced to him my grave misgivings', he said, 'first on the basis of my belief that Japan was already defeated and that dropping the bomb was completely unnecessary, and secondly because I thought that our country should avoid shocking world opinion by the use of a weapon whose employment was, I thought, no longer mandatory as a measure to save American lives.'

DECISION

'It is my opinion that the use of this barbarous weapon at Hiroshima and Nagasaki was of no material assistance in our war against Japan', wrote William Leahy, American chief of staff in his book, *I Was There* (1950). Truman was under pressure. He hesitated, then sent James F. 'Jimmy' Byrnes (later secretary of state) to talk to the people building the bomb. 'He returned to Washington with his recommendation', reported the *Daily Express* in the UK. 'It was: Do not use it. What caused them to change their mind is not known' (*Daily Express*, 7 August 1945). Truman later denied he was wavering: 'The final decision of where and when to use the atomic bomb was up to me. Let there be no mistake about it. I regarded the bomb as a military weapon and never had any doubt that it should be used.'

And so on 6 and 9 August 1945, Hiroshima and Nagasaki were destroyed by American atom bombs, and more than 360,000 Japanese civilians were killed (according to recent Japanese government statistics). On hearing the news, Albert Einstein, a lifelong pacifist, said: 'If I had only known, I would have been a locksmith.'

The awesome power of nuclear weapons as demonstrated at Hiroshima was confirmed over the postwar years as test followed test. Here the stern of the USS. *Nevada* is severely damaged by an atomic weapon tested at Bikini Atoll in 1951.

THE COLD WAR

During the cold war, nuclear weapons proliferated on both sides of the Iron Curtain. The Soviet Union and the USA began to build huge arsenals of atomic weapons. Britain and France developed their own nuclear capability. More – and more powerful – bombs were tested, and the tests polluted the Earth's atmosphere with radioactivity. But these tests did not go unchallenged in the free world. Ordinary people from all walks of life organised protests against the tests, with Japan – the first and only victim of nuclear attack – taking the lead. Similar protests followed in Great Britain and the United States with people from all religions and across the political spectrum taking part. By the mid-1950s a loose coalition of antinuclear groups had formed. The 'ban the bomb' movement had begun.

Defence and dissent

No sooner had Hiroshima and Nagasaki been devastated than Britain and Russia began to develop their own nuclear weapons and, on 22 September 1949, the Soviet Union exploded its first atomic bomb. Britain exploded its first A-bomb off the northwest coast of Australia, on 3 October 3 1952. Then on 1 March 1954, the United States set off the first-ever hydrogen bomb at Bikini Atoll in the Pacific. The 10-megaton hydrogen bomb was equal in power to 10 million tons of high explosives, more than the total of all the explosives used by both sides in World War II.

The fallout, which was much greater than predicted, affected hundreds of Marshall Islanders and engulfed the crew of the unfortunately named *Lucky Dragon*, a Japanese fishing vessel. By the time the little boat docked, all of the crew were suffering from radiation sickness, and one died shortly after, providing the catalyst needed to jump-start the Japanese antinuclear movement. In 1960, France also became an atomic power, testing its first bomb in the Algerian desert. These tests were all above ground, releasing radiation into the atmosphere and increasing the level of background radiation absorbed by everyone on the planet.

The public was suddenly made aware of the hazards of nuclear testing. New technical-sounding terms entered everyday language: 'radioactive iodine' that could enter the bones of growing children, 'strontium 90' that could contaminate children's milk with radioactivity, 'fallout', and 'radiation sickness'.

The Geiger counter became a familiar object in television shows with its sinister clicking. The seemingly uncontrolled atmospheric testing of atomic weapons by more and more countries caused widespread concern. When President Truman announced on 30 November 1950, that he would be prepared to use atomic bombs during the Korean War, it seemed only a matter of time before nuclear war was unleashed.

DUCK AND COVER

In the USA people built bomb shelters in their suburban backyards, city bomb shelters were designated by a yellow sign usually leading to a basement, and schoolchildren were shown how to hide under their desks in the event of an attack (chanting 'duck and cover', they were taught that covering their eyes and hiding under their desks would save them from an H-bomb).

On 28 November 1951, a 10-minute atomic defence drill in New York City started at 10:33 A.M. when sirens brought all five boroughs to a standstill. Twelve thousand police and 300,000 civil defence volunteers tested their procedures in the exercise. As sirens sounded, kids ducked and covered, office workers made their way to the designated shelters in the basements of buildings or in the subways, and the streets were quickly cleared. Anyone not participating in the mandatory exercise was arrested. There were a small number of peace protesters taken into custody for defying the order to take cover during what was the largest American Civil Defence exercise ever conducted. It originated the much-used quip about what to do when the sirens sound: 'Bend over. Put your head between your legs. Kiss your ass goodbye.'

Four years later, on 15 June 1955, the exercise was repeated in New York — and this time there were more antiwar protesters, and they were

American school-children practising a 'duck and cover' drill in their classroom in 1951 in preparation for a nuclear attack.

In early rumblings of the cold war, anti-Soviet pickets, representing exiles from Eastern Bloc countries, protested against a 1949 peace conference in New York, calling it 'a sounding board for Soviet propaganda'.

'Someday they'll give a war
and nobody will come.'

– CARL SANDBURG

'Mankind needs peace more than ever, for our entire planet, threatened by nuclear war, is in danger of total destruction. A destruction only man can provoke, only man can prevent.'

— ELIE WIESEL

A lone traffic cop stands on New York's Fifth Avenue during an atomic defence drill that brought Manhattan to a standstill for ten minutes in November 1951. Involving 12,000 police, and 11,000 firemen, it was the biggest such exercise in the history of the USA.

better organised. About 30 people gathered in a small park outside city hall and refused to take shelter when the sirens wailed. The police quickly moved in and arrested them all, including Living Theatre cofounders, Judith Malina and Julian Beck.

Malina remembered: 'I was sent to Bellevue for sassing the judge. The trial (with lawyers from the Ford Foundation's 20th Fund) was prolonged. We were an all-star set of defendants: Hugh Corbin (poet), Dorothy Day (founder of the Catholic Worker Movement), Ralph DiGia (War Resisters League founding member), Ammon Hennacy (a pacifist Christian anarchist who never paid taxes), Jackson Mac Low (poet and playwright), A. J. Muste (adviser to Martin Luther King, Jr.), James Peck (journalist and civil rights activist), and Bayard Rustin (civil rights activist, adviser to Martin Luther King, Jr.).' Many of these became important antiwar activists. They brought the idea of active resistance to the spread of nuclear weapons to a wider audience – one that was growing rapidly around the world.

BUNKER MENTALITY

In Britain many towns, such as the City of Coventry in 1954, disbanded their civil defence committees knowing that there was nothing they could do in the event of a nuclear attack except count the dead. The city had already seen severe conventional bombing and knew that in the event of a nuclear attack, hiding under the desk was not going to stop one's eyes from boiling in one's head. Throughout the decade the British government secretly built dozens of 'Regional Seats of Government' in order to save civil servants in the event of nuclear war.

Innocuous-looking buildings with steep roofs, which hid deep shafts leading to fully-equipped underground bunkers, began to appear nationwide. However, since entrance buildings were all the same, once peace protesters found the first, the rest were easily identified. In the early 1960s, demonstrations by the Committee of 100 outside these bunkers caused some of the most violent confrontations between police and protesters. Such skirmishes became more common as more people began to resist the threat of nuclear devastation.

After the euphoria of victory over the Germans and Japanese had subsided, the horrific reality of what had happened to the civilian populations of Hiroshima and Nagasaki began to sink in among the general populations of the 'victorious' countries. At universities visiting lecturers would project ghastly photographs of burn victims and show photographs of the shadow of a man or woman standing against a wall with a ladder, the only thing left after they had been vaporized by the blast, and the similar image of a shadow on stone steps, the person having vanished in an instant. People began to realise that this was what the politicians were talking about; the instant destruction of huge civilian populations, hundreds of thousands of lives snuffed out in a matter of minutes. The effect of seeing what a nuclear blast really did was traumatic, whether or not you agreed with the arms race or believed in nuclear weapons. A common fear touched the whole population, making the 1950s truly the age of anxiety.

PEACE PLEDGE UNION

The Peace Pledge Union (PPU) was born in Britain in 1934 as a response to the failure of the 1919 Peace Treaty and growing anxiety that Europe was drifting into another war, becoming the oldest secular pacifist organisation in Britain. (In 1937 it fused with the No More War movement, founded in 1921.) It was founded by Canon Dick Sheppard, an Anglican priest, following a huge response to a letter published in the *Guardian* newspaper (then the *Manchester Guardian*), in which he invited people to send him a postcard making a pledge to 'renounce war and never again to support another'.

Its members formally pledge: 'War is a crime against humanity. I renounce war, and am therefore determined not to support any kind of war. I am also determined to work for the removal of all causes of war.' Membership grew quickly; first tens of thousands, then hundreds of thousands by the start of World War II. Among its supporters were Lord Bertrand Russell (Nobel laureate in Literature), Vera Brittain (English writer, feminist, and pacifist), Aldous Huxley (English writer), Siegfried Sassoon (English poet and author), George Lansbury (British politician and socialist), and the Rev. Donald Soper (prominent Methodist minister and socialist). Later the composers Michael Tippett and Benjamin Britten became active members.

CONSCIENTIOUS OBJECTORS

The first major PPU campaign was against the Spanish Civil War, followed by protests against preparations for another war with Germany. PPU members were conscientious objectors during the war, who disinfected air-raid shelters during the blitz and helped rehabilitate people whose homes had been destroyed and whose family members had been killed or injured. To be a

An American Civil Defence recruiting poster from 1951, reminding a fearful public that, 'It *can* happen Here'.

It *can* happen Here

JOIN

CIVIL DEFENSE

A cartoon treatment of the 'duck and cover' Civil Defence campaign that appeared in a 1950s' animated movie.

'conscie' during World War II was hardly a passive position; they encountered much disapproval, they were attacked on the streets, and often faced disgrace from their own family and friends.

Virtually the only support they received was from *Peace News*, the weekly tabloid newspaper, subtitled 'The International Pacifist Weekly', first published in 1936 'to serve all who are working for peace'. After 1945 the people involved in *Peace News* remained at the centre of the fight against militarism and, along with members of the PPU (often the same people), were the first to protest against nuclear weapons.

It was only natural that in 1958 the first-ever march to Aldermaston – the British government's secret atomic weapons facility – was organised in the *Peace News* offices. In the years before that, however, various other organisations were formed, most of which finally merged in 1958 as the Campaign for Nuclear Disarmament.

In 1950, before Britain had successfully tested its atomic bomb, 100 scientists in Cambridge had petitioned the UK government to halt atomic weapons development, and on the anniversary of the bombing of Hiroshima, Rev. Donald Soper preached a sermon on the subject to a gathering of over 3,000 members of religious organisations in Trafalgar Square in London. That same year, the British Peace Committee (BPC), which included the Dean of Canterbury among its members, collected a million signatures for the Stockholm Peace Appeal, which called for 'an absolute ban on atomic weapons and weapons of mass destruction', but in both cases they were brushed aside by politicians, claiming that the BPC was too closely associated with the Communist-dominated World Peace Committee.

OPERATION GANDHI

In 1951 the PPU called for direct action: for a withdrawal of US forces from Britain, and the halt to Britain's manufacturing of atomic weapons. A dozen activists from their nonviolence commission launched Operation Gandhi.

THE LUCKY DRAGON INCIDENT

Eight years after American nuclear testing in the Marshall Islands began, at 6:45 A.M. on 1 March 1954, the 23-man crew of the Japanese fishing boat *Daigo Fukuryu Maru*, or *Lucky Dragon*, were shocked to see dawn apparently breaking in the west. 'The sky in the west suddenly lit up and the sea became brighter than day', a crew member recalled. 'We watched the dazzling light, which felt heavy. Seven or eight minutes later there was a terrific sound like an avalanche. Then a visible multicoloured ball of fire appeared on the horizon.' What they saw was the detonation of a bomb code-named Bravo on the island of Bikini. Their vessel was located 190 km (118 miles) east northeast of the explosion site, 32 km (20 miles) outside the US exclusion zone.

Fifteen minutes later a light rain began to fall, bringing with it thick white dust. Bravo was the equivalent of 17 megatons of TNT, 1,300 times the power of the bomb at Hiroshima, and designed to create a mass of lethal fallout.

By night everyone on board was ill, suffering from radiation sickness. It took the boat two weeks to return to port, where they were all treated for radiation burns for about a year. The radio operator, Aikichi Kuboyama, died seven months later of kidney failure caused by radiation.

At least 239 Marshall Islanders on the islands of Rongelap and Utrik, roughly 100 and 300 miles from Bikini, were exposed to radiation, as well as 28 Americans who were also well outside the exclusion zone. A total of 855 other boats were exposed to radiation, and all the fish they caught had to be destroyed.

The incident triggered the Japanese peace movement, provoking anti-American feelings on a number of levels: insensitivity to Japanese suffering in World War II, disruption to Japan's essential supply of fish, and a belief that the USA was developing atomic weapons and testing them with complete disregard for the population of the Pacific. By August 1955 a petition against US nuclear tests had been signed by 32 million people, and was presented that month at the first world conference against nuclear weapons held in Hiroshima.

The funeral procession for *Lucky Dragon* radioman, Aikichi Koboyama, makes its way through the streets of Tokyo to a ceremony attended by American Embassy Minister, J. Graham Parsons, who delivered the eulogy. The fisherman's widow, Suzo, carries an urn containing her late husband's ashes, walking behind a man bearing a portrait of Aikichi.

The members of Operation Gandhi believed that nonviolent action, like that of Gandhi in the struggle for Indian independence, could be used in Britain against war and nuclear weapons. They believed it might be necessary to break the law in these actions, and all the members declared that they were prepared for the adverse publicity, the likelihood of losing their jobs, and the possibility of spending time in jail in the furtherance of their beliefs. The secretary of Operation Gandhi was Hugh Brock, a wartime conscientious objector who had joined the staff of *Peace News* in the late 1940s as assistant editor.

On 11 January 1952, ten activists, led by Brock, staged a demonstration at the War Office in Whitehall. At 12 noon they walked up the steps of the War Office and sat down, blocking the door. They had informed the police of their intention in advance, so reinforcements were waiting in the building. The two policemen on duty whistled for their colleagues, and the demonstrators were pulled back to the pavement. Twice they returned to sit and block the entrance. After the third time, they were bundled into a police van and taken to Cannon Row Police Station. One woman who arrived late, asked a policeman where the War Office was, sat on the steps, and was immediately taken to join the other ten. Their protest received no press coverage but caused quite a large crowd to gather and had, at least, gone according to plan. So the members began to discuss their next move.

ALDERMASTON
Hugh Brock was now the editor of *Peace News*, and his newsroom was filled with details and gossip of the government's nuclear ambitions. Fellow pacifist, Jack Salkind, something of a collector of bus timetables, had noticed that there was a bus going to a place without a name, indicated only by the initials AWRE. It was near the small West Berkshire village of Aldermaston.

Wearing protective glasses, observers sit in rows, cinema-style, to watch a nuclear test explosion in the 1950s.

Hugh Brock was immediately suspicious and thought it might be one of the government's secret arms factories. He took a bus to the unnamed destination and reported back to the members of Operation Gandhi. To the south of the tiny village, within easy driving distance of Reading, was an enormous guarded complex of buildings and bunkers. The letters stood for Atomic Weapons Research Establishment (AWRE). Brock said it was huge. He had walked all the way around the perimeter and estimated it to be about 7 miles (11 km). There were several gates. Even to sit down and block the main gate would require at least 50 activists, and they had insufficient numbers to mount such a demonstration. Instead, they decided to distribute leaflets to the workers at midday when they left the plant at lunchtime.

They hired a bus from London, and nearly 30 protesters walked the 3 miles (5 km) to the main gate. The local police warned them: 'We can do nothing to protect you. There are more than a thousand workers down there'. But the workers were not hostile. They were interested in discussing the issues, and the demonstration concluded with an open-air meeting in Falcon Field, Aldermaston's small village green.

Operation Gandhi staged several more protests at Aldermaston as the Non-Violence Resistance Group, to distinguish themselves from the larger, Peace Pledge Union, because not all PPU members approved of their direct action.

THE PROTESTS GROW

As the arms race increased, so did the number of protest groups in the UK. In April 1954, the National H-Bomb Committee, led by six Labour Party MPs, met 300 representatives from church, work, and peace organisations and encouraged them to collect a million signatures on a petition – which only called on the government to conduct top-level disarmament talks with other world leaders, something that the government could easily ignore because disarmament talks

The 1955 atomic test site at Yucca Flat, Nevada, included a life-size hamlet dubbed Doom Town, complete with 'families' of mannequins, in order for scientists to observe the effects of the blast on a typical American small town.

were already a stated part of its agenda, though not one it was prepared to activate. The following year, Gertrude Fishwick, a retired civil servant and former suffragette, set up the Golders Green Committee for the Abolition of Nuclear Weapons Tests, probably the first grass-roots organisation created by concerned members of the community at large. They marched around Golders Green and Hampstead, where they were politely received.

THE RUSSELL APPEAL
In July 1955, Albert Einstein was a cosignatory of an appeal drafted by Lord Bertrand Russell, calling upon scientists worldwide to work for peace. The document described the massive genetic damage caused by nuclear radiation and concluded: 'Shall we put an end to the human race, or shall mankind renounce war?' It was signed by eleven prominent scientists (including nine Nobel laureates: Max Born, Percy W. Bridgman, Albert Einstein, Leopold Infeld, Frédéric Joliot-Curie, Herman J. Muller, Linus Pauling, Cecil F. Powell, Joseph Rotblat, Bertrand Russell, and Hideki Yukawa) and was delivered to the public on 9 July 1955, at a press conference held in Caxton Hall, London.

Known as the Russell-Einstein Manifesto, it was the genesis of the International Pugwash Conference, which meets to this day. The appeal argued on an intellectual level that was hard for politicians to ignore, but ignore it they did.

On 7 February 1957, the National Council for the Abolition of Nuclear Weapons Tests (NCANWT) was formed in London under the chairmanship of a Quaker, Arthur Goss. One of its first actions was to organise a women's protest march on 12 May, three days before the first British H-Bomb test. The interest in banning the tests was so strong that by the autumn they had 116 affiliated groups spread across the country, organising public meetings, marches, and film shows, and distributing leaflets. The rising levels of radiation in the atmosphere as a

result of atomic tests and fear of the devastation that nuclear warfare would unleash had led to widespread concern among the general population. Members of NCANWT came from all walks of life, from factory workers to religious leaders, politicians to mothers anxious about their children's future.

DIRECT ACTION
In April, the Emergency Committee for Direct Action Against Nuclear War was formed by author and medical professional, Alex Comfort; Bertrand Russell; Hugh Brock; peace activist, Pat Arrowsmith; Irish comedian, writer and musician, Spike Milligan; and other activists, to raise funds to send a group of their members – Harold and Sheila Steele, Reginald Reynolds and others – into the bomb-testing area in the Pacific as a way of stopping the tests. This was direct action at its most dangerous. Unfortunately, the test had already occurred by the time Harold Steele and his party arrived, because the government had thrown bureaucratic obstacles in their way, but the trip was widely reported in the press.

There had long been activists within Britain's Labour Party and, in the summer of 1957, they formed the Labour H-Bomb Campaign Committee and organised a rally of 4,000 people in Trafalgar Square that September. There were now so many groups, many more than those listed above, that it became obvious that they would be much more effective if they were all part of a mass movement, so the Campaign for Nuclear Disarmament was proposed.

THE BIRTH OF CND
In November 1957, English writer and broadcaster, J. B. Priestley, wrote an article for the *New Statesman* entitled, 'Britain and the Nuclear Bombs', which drew such a massive response from readers that the editor, Kingsley Martin, suggested the time was right for a mass movement to oppose nuclear weapons. The National Council for the Abolition of Nuclear

A pre-CND 'ban the bomb' demonstration held in London, in mid-1957, was organised by the British Peace Committe and the British Communist Party.

Weapons Tests already had offices and staff, as well as over 100 affiliated groups, so it seemed logical that they should become the base for a nationwide organisation. A meeting was arranged on 28 January 1958, in the house of John Collins, canon of St Paul's Cathedral. Although there was disagreement on how to achieve their aim, the various groups ultimately decided to combine efforts. They would call themselves the Campaign for Nuclear Disarmament. The philosopher Bertrand Russell was to be president; J. B. Priestley was the vice president; Canon Collins was the chairman; and Peggy Duff, an organiser for NCANWT, became the organising secretary.

The next day the executive committee of NCANWT met to vote itself out of existence and pass all its facilities and funds to the newly formed CND, which now set up in their offices at 146 Fleet Street, London. On the committee was British journalist, James Cameron, the only one to have actually witnessed an atomic test and to have toured Hiroshima after the blast. Other members included Member of Parliament, Michael Foot, Arthur Goss, the previous chair of NCANWT, and Kingsley Martin, editor of the *New Statesman*.

MISSION STATEMENT

The new organisation presented itself to the public at a meeting held at Central Hall, Westminster, across the square from the Houses of Parliament, on 17 February 1958. Interest was so high that more than 3,000 people clamoured to get in, and three other halls in the building had to be quickly requisitioned. The speakers, including Lord Bertrand Russell, operated in shifts, rotating from hall to hall to deliver their message to the packed assemblies. The Campaign for Nuclear Disarmament distributed a press release that read:

> The purpose of the campaign is to demand a British initiative to reduce the nuclear peril and stop the armaments race, if need be by unilateral action by Great Britain. As a first step towards a general disarmament convention, Britain should press for negotiations at top level on the following issues:
> 1. The stopping of all further tests of nuclear weapons.
> 2. The stopping of the establishment of new missile bases.
> 3. The securing of the establishment of neutral and nuclear-free zones.
> 4. The securing of the abolition of the manufacture and stockpiling of nuclear weapons.
> 5. The prevention of the acquisition of nuclear weapons by other nations.
> In order to underline the sincerity of her own initiative, Britain should be prepared to announce that, pending negotiations, she will suspend patrol flights of airplanes equipped with nuclear weapons; she will make no further tests of hydrogen bombs; she will not proceed with the establishment of missile bases on her territory; she will not provide nuclear weapons to any country.

In brief there was a shift from just campaigning against the testing of nuclear weapons to opposing the weapons themselves. The CND called for nothing less than an end to the military use of nuclear energy. Only then would the future of the planet be secure. Britain was not the only country where people felt moved to demonstrate their outrage at the threat of nuclear destruction. Similar groups had arisen in the USA, Japan, and other countries.

As yet, there was no universal symbol to represent their views. Peace, as a concept, was often shown as a dove, but unfortunately, the peace dove drawn by Picasso was given by him to the French Communist Party and consequently came laden with too much political and historical baggage. Besides, it was hard to draw and unsuitable as graffiti. Fortunately, someone had been giving the matter some serious thought.

As in Britain, antinuclear and antiwar groups flourished in the USA from the early 1950s onwards. This demonstration at the White House in 1955 against President Eisenhower's Formosa policy was organised by various pacifist groups, including the War Resisters League, the Catholic Worker movement, and Peacemakers.

HAPPY BIRTHDAY, PEACE SYMBOL

In Britain scores of small antinuclear test groups came together in January 1958 to form the Campaign for Nuclear Disarmament (CND). One of these small groups, the Direct Action Committee Against Nuclear War, had already planned a march from London to Aldermaston, where the British government developed nuclear weapons. But with the CND getting unprecedented publicity, and the whole nuclear debate suddenly becoming high profile, the Aldermaston march took on the appearance of a major mass protest. The organisers asked one of their members, a textile designer named Gerald Holtom, to devise banners and signs for the event. Holtom came up with the peace symbol, starting with the British naval semaphore signs for N and D, standing for Nuclear Disarmament. Over the years it has become a universal logo for peace.

A sign of the times

While the CND was being set up, another organisation had been making plans for action. The Direct Action Committee against Nuclear War (DAC), which had sent Harold Steele to Tokyo, bound for the Pacific, met in November 1957 to discuss its next move. Hugh Brock, the editor of *Peace News,* who had organised the first demonstration at Aldermaston back in 1952, suggested that the DAC arrange a four-day march to the atomic weapons factory for Easter 1958. The DAC members were mostly from an anarchist-pacifist background and, like Brock, were influenced by Mahatma Gandhi's pacifist fight for Indian independence.

They were determined to use his nonviolent principles in their campaign to rid Britain and the world of nuclear weapons. Their intention was to tackle the problem head-on; to bypass the politicians and engage the attention of workers at the AWRE directly, to try to convince them to stop working on weapons of mass destruction. However, unlike the 1952 demonstration, this one would be preceded by a march that they hoped would focus attention on the issue so that people at Aldermaston would be ready for the debate when the DAC marchers arrived.

An ad hoc Aldermaston march committee was set up, comprising Member of Parliament, Frank Allaun, Hugh Brock from *Peace News,* Walter Wolfgang, organiser of the Labour Party's H-Bomb Campaign Committee, and Michael Randle, who was in charge of promoting *Peace News.* Meetings were held every week or so in the House of Commons, in a committee room that Frank Allaun would book for them. There, surrounded by heraldic wallpaper and Victorian panelling, they debated how to change policies made in similar rooms in the same building.

The CND had only existed for a few days and had not yet held its first public meeting, so DAC was cautious when asked if they wanted to be involved with the march. The members agreed to give their blessing to the march ... 'but should make it clear at this stage of the Campaign that

they could not be very closely involved'. The DAC march committee had originally envisioned about 50 or 60 people walking all 53 miles (85 km) from London to Aldermaston, but with the launch of CND and all the attendant publicity, it now seemed that many more people would be coming. Many members of the Labour Party were sympathetic and intended to march, including members of parliament; a number of trade unions intended to march, bringing with them their magnificent banners.

The Universities and Left Review club, which included people involved with the forerunner of the *New Left Review,* formed a contingent, as did the Victory for Socialism group. The Quakers were the largest religious group and planned to march from the go, but many other Christian organisations became involved. The committee realised that things had changed, and several hundred people could be expected to attend.

BANNERS AGAINST THE BOMB
This changed the nature of the demonstration, making a change of policy necessary: The original idea of calling upon the staff at Aldermaston to stop working there was now overshadowed by the potential size of the march. The committee was divided, with Hugh Brock and Michael Randle remaining in favour of addressing the workers, and Frank Allaun and Walter Wolfgang

Rain-soaked protesters on the 1958 Aldermaston march carry the semaphore peace sign for the first time in a public demonstration.

now opposed to the idea. In a compromise the march was followed by a nine-week picket of the Aldermaston bomb factory, during which the workers were asked to withdraw their labour.

Given the enlarged size of the march, the issue of banners became of prime importance. The whole point, after all, was to express their views with leaflets and conversations; banners and slogans were a key part of the mix if they wanted people to know all the players as they marched through the streets.

GERALD HOLTOM

A member of the Direct Action Committee's Twickenham branch, textile designer, Gerald Holtom, was involved in the planning of the march from the beginning. Because he ran his own graphic design studio, he was given the role of designing the banners and placards to be carried to Aldermaston. Holtom was a committed Christian and pacifist; he was tall and softly spoken. He graduated from the Royal College of Art in 1935. His deeply felt pacifism led him to spend World War II working on a farm in Norfolk as a conscientious objector. Holtom took his responsibility for getting the peace message across seriously. He wanted to create a design style that was not only informative but also one that summed up the message – something that these days might be called a 'brand'.

Holtom was best known for appliqué work rather than graphic art. He made the striking covering for the east wall of Sir Basil Spence's 1957 St. Oswald's Church in Tile Hill, Coventry, but his most famous work was the appliqué altar cloths and sequence of acoustic panels on the west end of St Paul's Church, Lorrimore Square in south London, built in 1959–1960 to replace a Victorian church bombed during the war.

The American religious right later tried to suggest that whoever designed the peace symbol must have been a devil-worshipping communist, but Gerald Holtom was as far from this stereotype as humanly possible.

One of Gerald Holtom's original sketches shows how he imagined the various banners might appear on the planned march to Aldermaston, including cross symbols for the Christian groups and his new semaphore-based 'ND' logo.

The unborn child.

Ilhs : Elk

In medieval symbolism the modern peace sign without its circle represents a dead man, part of a visual shorthand for the many vicissitudes of family life. There are signs for birth, death, pregnancy, friendship, quarrels and so on. In order to make the peace symbol represent the so-called broken cross, you have to regard it as a rune. Runes were a system designed by the Goths using Greek and Latin cursive script. By the 4th century they had spread to Germany and other Teutonic countries, and in north Germany a system of magic evolved, although the magical properties of each rune were known to just a few people.

The peace sign, if it is turned upside down and the circle removed, resembled the runic symbol *alhs* or *algiz*, which is like a man standing with arms upstretched, and means 'elk'. It is a glyphic signage of an elk's horns and head as seen from the front. Despite the theories of extremist opponents to the peace movement, only by a leap of the imagination can this be made to mean 'life'. And only by an even greater leap can you infer that inverted it will bring death. If used

magically, it would have been used the correct way up, presumably enabling one to do some damage, or good, to another man's elk.

There is a traditional use of the peace symbol (without its circle) in the Christian religion, still in use today. The grapevine cross, dating from the 4th century, is used extensively by the Georgian Orthodox Church. It is sometimes called the Georgian cross or St Nino's cross and has its arms drooping a little – 30 degrees rather than the peace symbol's 45 degrees. St Nino, a Cappadocian woman who preached Christianity in Georgia, is said to have forged the cross herself on her way to Mtskheta, near Tbilisi, and secured the two arms by entwining them upright with her own hair, which is why it droops.

A German publisher once wrote to Bertrand Russell complaining that the peace symbol was a death symbol because the arms pointed downwards. 'I am afraid that I cannot follow your argument that the ND badge is a death symbol', Russell replied. 'It was invented by a member of our movement as the badge of the Direct Action Committee against Nuclear War,

Man

The man dies.

for the first Aldermaston march. It was designed from the naval code of semaphore, and the symbol represents the code letters for ND. To the best of my knowledge, the Navy does not employ signallers who work upside down.'

However, attempts to discredit the symbol have not stopped. In 2005, Alan Scholl, the director of Mission and Campaigns for the right-wing American John Birch Society wrote: 'The real mystery of the peace symbol is why a group of peace activists in the late 1950s would knowingly adopt a symbol of death as a symbol for peace. One explanation is that they were strongly influenced by Marxist-Leninism and sought peace by the same means as Lenin. "As an ultimate objective, 'peace' simply means Communist world control", Lenin once wrote. As a revolutionary who had come to power in a bloody coup, Lenin firmly held that world control would come through bloody world revolution, in other words, through the deaths of thousands if not millions. For "peace" activists in the Leninist tradition, the peace symbol as death rune is, unfortunately, appropriate.'

This comes from an organisation that fought to retain segregation in Southern schools, that believed Britain, France and other imperial powers should retain their colonies, and who believed that Dwight D. Eisenhower, Franklin D. Roosevelt and Harry S. Truman were all part of a communist conspiracy to undermine the USA. Robert Welch, the founder of the society, wrote that President Eisenhower was a 'conscious, dedicated agent of the Communist Conspiracy' and, in 1956, claimed that other top government officials, such as John Foster Dulles and Allan W. Dulles, were 'communist tools'.

Nonetheless, the idea spread and is still common in parts of the USA. Many people in the peace movement were pleased to be attacked by the Birchites; to them it proved that they were doing the right thing. Although thoroughly discredited, in 1970, *Political Potpourri*, a national Republican Party newsletter, published a World War II Nazi propaganda poster featuring the Algiz rune, claiming that the peace symbol was somehow associated with death.

Internetional
Code flag N (Negative).

NUCLEAR DISARMA

NUCLEAR DISARMA

International
Code Flag D
("Keep out of my way.
I am manoeuvering with difficulty!")

In this sketch that
Holtom presented
to the fledgling CND,
he envisioned a variety
of banner designs
being displayed by the
Aldermaston marchers.

A. J. MUSTE, AMERICAN PEACE ACTIVIST

A.J. Muste, known simply as 'AJ' to his friends and colleagues, had worked with the American Civil Liberties Union back in the 1920s and was for several years the chairman of the Christian Pacifist organisation, the Fellowship of Reconciliation. Then came a period of radical Marxism: He was a founder member of the Conference for Progressive Labor Action (CPLA), which sought to reform the American Federation of Labor; then, as the Depression took hold in the USA, the CPLA became more revolutionary and was instrumental in the formation, in 1933, of the American Workers' Party. Throughout the 1930s Muste organised sit-down strikes and union actions moving ever further to the left. Eventually he merged his own group with that of James Cannon to form the Trotskyist Workers Party of America. Then he underwent a strange transformation.

In 1936, troubled by various aspects of Marxism-Leninism, he left the USA to visit Leon Trotsky in Norway. When he returned later that year, he had once more become a Christian pacifist. In 1940, he rejoined the Fellowship of Reconciliation as their executive secretary, and it was in this position that he campaigned from a pacifist position against the USA joining World War II. In 1942, with civil rights activists, Bayard Rustin and James Farmer, he formed the Congress On Racial Equality (CORE). In 1945, he helped to publish *Direct Action*, with activists David Dillinger and Dorothy Day, condemning the bombing of Hiroshima and Nagasaki. In 1953, at the age of 68, Muste claimed to 'retire', but that year he started the War Resister's League, which continues to this day. He became the leader of the Committee for Nonviolent Action and took part in many direct actions: sailing ships into nuclear test zones, cutting through or climbing over the perimeter fences of nuclear manufacturing sites and blocking the launch of nuclear submarines. He was involved with the 1961 peace march from San Francisco to Moscow and, thanks to his leftist background, he was able to persuade the Soviets into allowing them to march into Moscow's Red Square.

In possibly the most active period in his life Muste became a central figure in the coalition of groups and individuals that opposed the war in Vietnam. In 1966 he led a delegation of pacifists to Saigon, who were arrested and deported. Later that same year, he met with Ho Chi Minh in Hanoi, and less than four weeks later he died suddenly in New York City.

A. J. Muste poses with other members of the 1966 peace delegation to Hanoi. From the left, Communist theoretician and founder of Students for a Democratic Society, Herbert Aptheker; activist, Tom Hayden; Muste; and Yale history professor, Staughton Lynd.

Holtom was part of a quiet, pacifist element in the Church of England. After the war, they helped rebuild the churches that they saw as a focal point for communities, destroyed by the bombs. Many of those seeking to discredit the symbol thought that Bertrand Russell, noted for his left-leaning atheism, had designed it, which was also fiction.

PROTOTYPE

Towards the end of February 1958, Gerald Holtom arrived at the offices of *Peace News,* where the actual planning of the march was taking place. The practical organising was done by Hugh Brock and Michael Randle, from the March Committee, who were both on the staff of *Peace News*; Gene Sharp, a *Peace News* staff member, largely responsible for the Briefing Leaflet for the march; and Pat Arrowsmith. It was Randle, Brock and Arrowsmith who met Gerald Holtom to review his sketches. Under his arms Holtom carried two large rolls of heavy brown paper. One roll contained drawings of designs for banners for the march:

checkered flags, semaphore code flags, and Christian flags with crosses as well as a curious symbol that no one had seen before that he was proposing to represent the antinuclear campaign. He had drawn a line of marchers carrying these flags to show how the designs would look in use.

On the other roll of paper, he had made more detailed sketches of this new insignia, which he thought might be useful as a symbol for the march and the nuclear disarmament campaign. He had recognised early on that the biggest design difficulty was finding a shorthand way of expressing the lengthy slogan 'Unilateral Nuclear Disarmament'. His solution was a circle and within it the now familiar symbol, a cross with the horizontal arms pointing at 45 degree angles downwards. He explained to his small audience that the symbol was made up of the British navy semaphore letters for N and D. The semaphore system used two hand-held flags to spell out messages from one ship to another, provided that the signalmen were within telescope range.

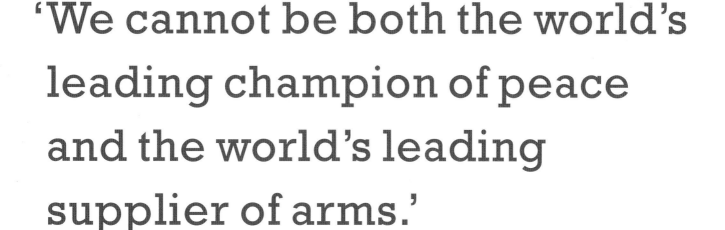

'We cannot be both the world's leading champion of peace and the world's leading supplier of arms.'

— JIMMY CARTER

GODZILLA AND NUCLEAR PARANOIA

Japanese reaction to Hiroshima and Nagasaki was clouded by the emotional turmoil of losing the war, American occupation, rebuilding and the beginnings of modern democracy. It took the *Lucky Dragon* incident in 1954, when Japanese fishermen fishing in international waters were exposed to deadly nuclear radiation from American thermonuclear testing, to focus the national consciousness on the need for peace and an end to nuclear testing. In addition to the contamination of the fish supplies in the Pacific, northern Japan had experienced radioactive rain caused by Russian nuclear testing. Japan felt abused by the careless attitude of the superpowers in their quest for weapons of mass destruction and a national nuclear paranoia became evident. One result of this was a series of antinuclear films, the best of which was *Gojira* (*Godzilla*), directed by Ichiro Honda.

Released in 1954, the film is largely based on the Lucky Dragon incident and opens with a Japanese fishing boat being overwhelmed by a nuclear blast – the same blast that awakens a long dormant dinosaur, Gojira, symbolising the destructive evil of nuclear weapons. In the original Japanese version, the eminent scientist, Dr Yamane, gives a speech warning that continued H-bomb testing will create more and more Gojiras. He warns that all nuclear testing must cease, or the world will pay a terrible price. In the mediocre American version, *Godzilla, King of the Monsters!,* which used only the shots of Godzilla and substituted American actors for Japanese, the ending has a voice-over with Raymond Burr explaining that Japan is now free from the menace of Godzilla forever. The original antiwar, antinuclear message was obliterated by cold-war propaganda.

The Godzilla movies went on to become the longest-running film series in cinema history and have also inspired many imitations such as *Gorgo* (1961) and *Gamera* (1965), though it was itself an imitation of *King Kong* (1933) and *The Beast from 20,000 Fathoms* (1953). As Dr. Yamane warned in the original film, if Godzilla is not destroyed completely, he will return again and again, and true to his prediction, Godzilla returns to destroy Tokyo again and again, and nuclear weapons are still with us.

A typically lurid poster for the U.S. version of the Godzilla movie, *Godzilla King of the Monsters,* in which the original antinuclear message was twisted to become a neat bit of cold war rhetoric.

In 1956, the company that created *Godzilla*, Toho Studios, came up with the flying monster, Rodan. The original Japanese name was Radon, but American distributors thought this might be confused with the atomic element of the same name.

THE FLYING MONSTER...
RODAN

Spawned amid seething Lava Beds!...

...hurling its 100 tons of terror across the stratosphere!...

...smashing Cities and sight,...

THE KING BROTHERS
present A TOHO PRODUCTION

a DCA release

print by TECHNICOLOR

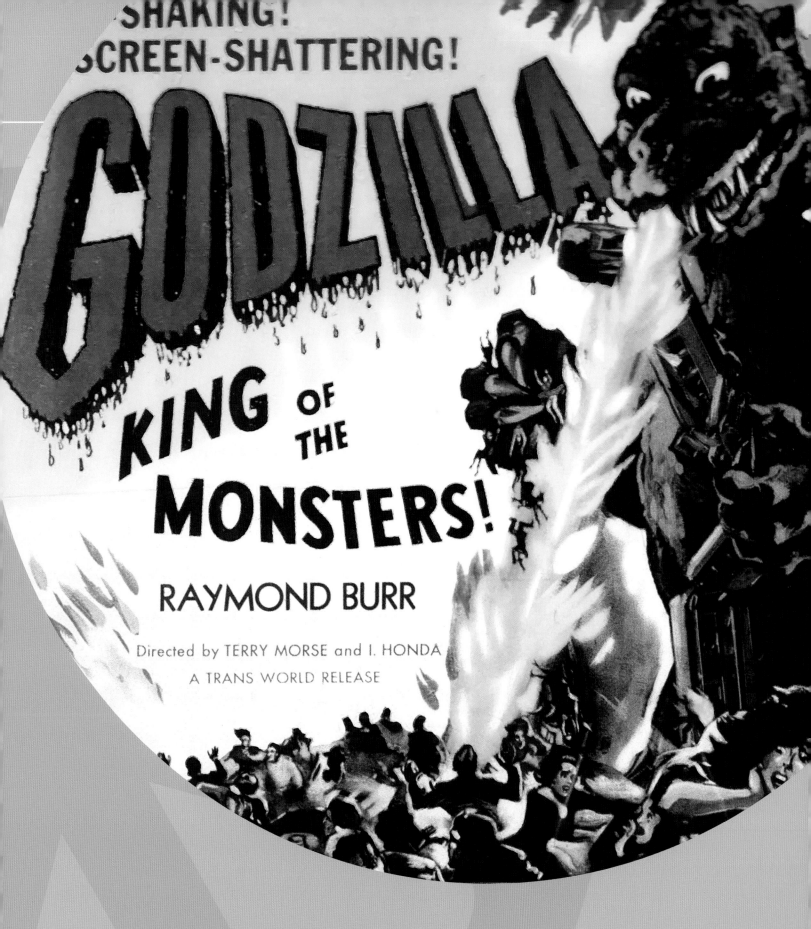

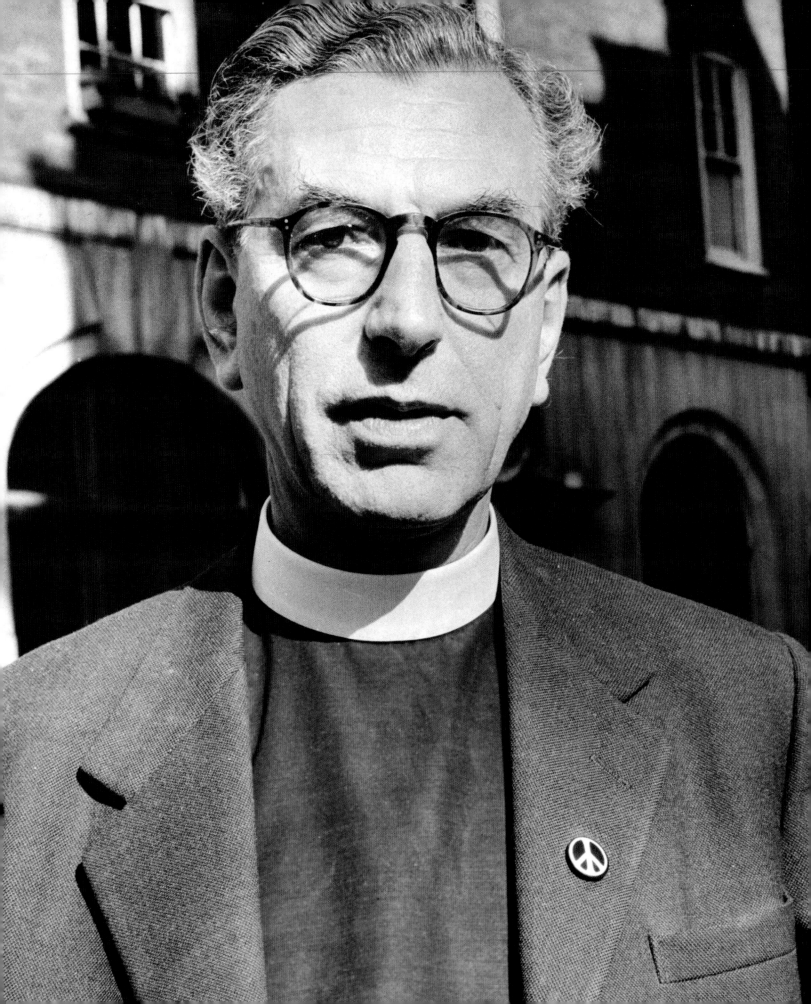

'We still have a choice today: non-violent co-existence or violent co-annihilation.'

— MARTIN LUTHER KING, JR

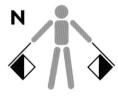

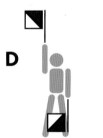

The semaphore signals that formed the basis of the peace sign – N above and D below.

Canon John Collins, peace activist and chairman of the Campaign for Nuclear Disarmament.

One flag held vertically and the other pointing directly down signified D, while two flags at 45 degrees from horizontal was N. The symbol embodied an encoded message calling for Nuclear Disarmament. He showed them versions in brown ink, with the circle superimposed on a brown square, and a version in purple ink. According to one report, the committee were initially dubious, but his arguments quickly won them over, and with only slight hesitation they decided to formally adopt the symbol and asked him to work on some preliminary designs.

Michael Randle, however, remembers their support for the symbol as being immediately positive. 'I recall particularly the day when a Twickenham artist, Gerald Holtom, arranged to see Hugh Brock, Pat Arrowsmith and myself in the small *Peace News* offices in Blackstock Road and showed us the enigmatic symbol he had designed and which he urged us to adopt', Randle wrote in *Campaigns for Peace*. 'He also brought sketches of how he envisaged the march, with long banners stretching across the road with his symbol at either end of it, and such was his enthusiasm and persuasiveness that we immediately agreed to his proposal. This was how the now famous nuclear disarmament

symbol came to be adopted.' Holtom himself remembered them being totally encouraging. In a letter to Hugh Brock in September 29, 1973, he said, 'Without you, Michael Randle and Pat, there would have been no symbol.'

DOUBTS

However, Holtom still had his own doubts about it. In the same letter to Brock, he wrote: 'The day after your unequivocal approval of the symbol, I made a badge the size of a sixpence in paper, black ink on white, pinned it on my lapel with some trepidation in fear of ridicule and forgot it.' Later that day, while visiting the local post office, a young woman behind the counter asked him about the badge he was wearing. He explained it was new and it called for nuclear disarmament. He later wrote that as he returned home, he was 'filled with embarrassment and doubts'. Michael Randle wrote: 'I think what enthused us was not so much the explanation of the genesis of the symbol, as the vision in his sketches of how the march might look if we adopted it.'

A week later Holtom arrived at the first meeting of what was to become the London Region CND, held in the small hall of St Pancras Town Hall. He brought with him some of the long banners he had devised for the upcoming march. At the back of the hall, he unrolled a bolt of black cloth about 6 yd- (5 m) long, designed to be carried sideways on the march so people could read them as they walked past, like an advert on the side of a bus. This provided another solution to conveying a lengthy slogan to the public. He fixed bamboo poles to each end and asked two people to hold them up. Written on the black cloth were the words 'Nuclear Disarmament' in white paint, and at each end was his curious new symbol, also in white. The results were striking. He explained to the meeting that it was the semaphore for the initials N and D, Nuclear Disarmament, but that the broken cross could also mean the death of man, whereas the circle symbolised the unborn child. In combination it represented the terrible threat nuclear weapons posed to humanity, including the unborn.

This explanation of the symbolism comes from Rudoph Koch's, *The Book of Signs*, which is almost certainly where Holtom got his inspiration. Koch's book, which contains almost 500 symbols from medieval Europe, was first published in Britain in 1930, but it was issued as a cheap paperback by Dover Publications in 1955 and became popular among art students at that time. As the director of a design studio, it is unlikely that Holtom did not have a copy. His explanation of the symbol for a dead man and the symbol for an unborn child match those of Koch precisely. The London Region CND was enthusiastic about his designs; they liked the stark black and white, which was easy to reproduce, and said they would like to use these designs on the march. They could not speak for CND itself.

OTHER SYMBOLS

The symbol was more than just a design problem to Holtom; he believed passionately in the campaign and had thought long and deeply about a symbol to represent it. Years later, in 1973, Holtom wrote to Hugh Brock, telling him of his state of mind at the time and explaining in

The original Aldermaston marchers leave London on the first day of their journey by foot over the Easter weekend in 1958.

greater detail the personal symbolism involved in his creation of the logo. For him it was not simply another design job – in fact, the intensity of his feelings on the subject may be what inspired him to the rarest of creations: a new symbol that would resonate across nations and generations, gathering meaning, until it became part of the human visual vocabulary.

At first he had thought of using the Christian cross as the dominant motif, but he told Brock that he realised 'in Eastern eyes the Christian Cross was synonymous with crusading tyranny culminating in Belsen and Hiroshima and the manufacture and testing of the H-bomb'. At the time, he had spoken with various priests about the idea, and they were not happy with using the cross on a protest march. He also rejected the image of the dove, then used extensively by the peace movement – in particular the one drawn for them by Picasso – as it had been appropriated by 'the Stalin regime ... to bless and legitimise their H-bomb manufacture'.

Holtom told Brock that on 21 February 1958, the day he designed the symbol, he was in despair. Deep despair. 'I drew myself: the representative of an individual in despair, with hands palm outstretched outward and downward in the manner of Goya's peasant before the firing squad in his painting, *The Third of May 1808*. I formalised the drawing into a line and put a circle around it ... . It was ridiculous at first and such a puny thing ... .'

Holtom claimed he was inspired by Goya's painting, *The Third of May 1808*, showing a peasant with arms outstretched in front of a firing squad.

In fact, Holtom may have been thinking of a different Goya. In *The Third of May 1808* the man before the firing squad has his hands raised high in the air, albeit in the same V position. However, one of the most famous images from Goya's *Disasters of War* series of 80 etchings is one of a peasant on his knees, slumped in depression, with his hands in exactly the position Holtom describes.

DISSATISFACTION

Holtom was not happy with his design: In many ways he was asking too much of himself. Everybody believed nuclear disarmament was desirable. He felt that it was not enough just to call for nuclear disarmament. He wanted a symbol that conveyed the need for individuals to take responsibility for the direct creative action that was necessary in order to combat the nuclear threat. As he saw it, the key to nuclear disarmament was unilateral action.

Holtom returned to his studio in Twickenham, fresh from meeting with Brock and the others at *Peace News*, and put his staff to work, silk-screening 'lollipop' signs and banners, all bearing his new design. Five hundred cardboard lollipop signs on sticks were made; half of them were black on white and half white on green. Holtom was a committed Christian and, as the Church's liturgical colours change over Easter 'from Winter to Spring, from Death to Life', he used the same symbolism for the banners.

Peter Sellers · George C. Scott

In Stanley Kubrick's

Dr. Strangelove

Or:
How
I Learned
To
Stop
Worrying
And
Love
The
Bomb

the hot-line suspense comedy

HOLLYWOOD'S NUCLEAR DOOM MOVIES

◀ Addressing the lunacy of the cold-war policy of 'mutual destruction', Stanley Kubrick's 1964 satire, *Dr Strangelove Or: How I Learned to Stop Worrying and Love the Bomb*, was a powerful indictment of the nuclear arms race, with Peter Sellers in no less than three roles; as the American President, a British air force officer and the sinister ex-Nazi bomb scientist Dr Strangelove.

The threat of nuclear annihilation was an ever-present fact of life in the USA in the 1950s and was inevitably reflected in Hollywood films. These ranged from 'realistic' dramas based on the real possibility of a nuclear war, to sci-fi fantasies in which the effects of radiation – as Japanese cinema had already demonstrated with Godzilla – produced monstrous mutations, usually in overgrown creatures that terrorized the populace.

The former end-of-the-world scenarios included the low-budget melodrama, *Five*, made in 1951, Harry Belafonte's man-alone-in-Manhattan role in *The World, the Flesh and the Devil* in 1959, and the Stanley Kramer-directed film, *On The Beach*, that same year.

On The Beach, based on a 1957 novel by Nevil Shute, certainly explored the subject most thoroughly, describing the months after a near-future nuclear war (set in 1964) had rendered all the Northern Hemisphere uninhabitable. Based in the southern Australian city of Melbourne, Gregory Peck's submarine commander sets out to America's west coast only to find no traces of life. Meanwhile, as the radiation clouds move south, some of the Melbourne populace prepare to live out their remaining days, while others line up outside the hospitals to receive their cyanide pills. A religious group hangs a sign across the front of city hall that reads: 'There Is Still Time, Brother'.

Radiation-created movie monsters ranged from the giant ants in *Them!* (1954), caused by atomic tests in the New Mexico desert, to Ray Bradbury's slumbering dinosaur in *The Beast from 20,000 Fathoms* (1953), in which the awakened colossus swam down from the atomic Arctic to take a rest in Coney Island.

But a more personalised angle was explored in *The Incredible Shrinking Man* (1957), in which, after sailing through a radioactive dust cloud (echoing the real-life *Lucky Dragon* incident of three years earlier), the hero finds he is shrinking by the day. A series of special-effect adventures, involving him being threatened by the family cat and subsequently a giant spider, lead to the point where he contemplates the universe as he faces the possibility of becoming no more than a simple atom ... the symbolic point from which his bizarre transformation had been artificially triggered in man's often irresponsible conquest of nature.

▶ Grant Williams confronts a spider in his role as the increasingly diminutive hero in Jack Arnold's *The Incredible Shrinking Man*, from a novel by Richard Matheson – who also wrote the screenplay.

THE DOVE OF PEACE

Issued by the Returning Servicemen's Association (RSA) to commemorate the signing of the Versaille Peace Treaty in 1919, this button marked the true end of World War I. Despite the armistice having been signed on 11 November 1918, the Treaty signing on 28 June marked the official cessation of violence between the warring countries. The RSA, established to aid the passage of veterans back to their homeland and funded by voluntary as well as governmental aid, sold the button to raise funds.

The dominant image of the world has areas marked in red, showing those areas that were still part of the British Empire, and where thousands of men were sent to their death in the conflict.

The dove that flies over the world has the word 'peace' in its beak, rather than the usual olive branch. A white dove bearing the olive branch had been a recognised Christian and Judaic symbol of peace and is derived from the story of Noah sending a bird to find a sign of hope. Picasso famously chose to paint a white dove (without the olive branch) to mark the International Peace Congress in Paris, in 1949.

The black-and-white lollipops were to be carried on Good Friday and Saturday, whereas on Easter Sunday and Monday the green-and-white ones were distributed. His design called for thin arms on the cross culminating in a serif where they met the enclosing circle. Many variations on this theme have been tried over the years, but this design remains the most elegant. Holtom still felt his design didn't say enough.

A 'REVOLUTION OF THOUGHT'

Nonetheless, he turned his energies to making the banners and lollipop signs for the march. A few days later, in his workshop, he experienced a 'revolution of thought'. He told Brock in his letter that he had been holding the symbol in his hand, turning it around, staring at it 'in the struggle to find a way beyond despair'. It was then that it suddenly occurred to him that if the symbol was inverted, then it could be seen as representing the tree of life, the tree on which Jesus Christ had been crucified, and that, for Christians like Gerald Holtom, was a symbol of hope and resurrection.

Even better, the inverted image of a figure with arms stretched upward and outward was the semaphore signal for U: unilateral. And so for Holtom the symbol took on an even more symbolic meaning. Just as the American religious right later claimed that the design was an inverted cross, Holtom inverted the design to become a symbol of hope.

Holtom also made the lead banners for the march, the biggest of which read: 'March from

London to Aldermaston' in the striking white letters on a black background, flanked by the peace symbol. The banner was used every year, though the lettering was changed to read 'March to London from Aldermaston' after the first year. Each year it was brought out, cleaned up, and a fresh bunch of daffodils attached to it as a symbol of spring and life. Its stark black-and-white design was modern-looking at the time, and provided a template for antinuclear posters and banners in Britain for years to come.

THE BAN-THE-BOMB BADGE

The march also needed badges, both for the marchers and to distribute and sell. Using Gerald Holtom's design, Eric Austin of Kensington CND stamped them from clay and fired them in a kiln. They were white, with the circle and cross in black, and were distributed with a note pointing out that these ceramic badges would be one of the few human artefacts likely to withstand a nuclear attack unless they received a direct nuclear hit, the only evidence that a living person had once stood where it was found. Austin echoed Holtom's reference to Rudolph Koch's, *The Book of Signs*, by stating that the

symbol had several layers of meaning embodied in it: both the semaphore for N and D and also the traditional symbols of life and death. 'The gesture of despair had long been associated with the death of man and the circle with the unborn child', he said.

After the original ceramic badges, which have now become collectors' items, the Campaign made a large batch in plastic before settling on cheap mass-produced tin badge, with the symbol in white on black, which became the standard design. The design was brilliant, easy to draw and graffiti. But there were still doubters, as Michael Randle later wrote, recalling when the first pamphlet was printed bearing the symbol.

'IT WILL NEVER CATCH ON'

A veteran peace activist complained to Randle that he and the others on the committee must have been out of their minds in adopting it. Randle reports his friend saying: 'What on Earth were you, Hugh and Pat thinking about when you adopted that symbol? It doesn't mean a thing and it will never catch on.' As Randle points out, had the march not been a success, his friend would probably have been proved right.

'You never need an argument against the use of violence, you need an argument for it.'

– NOAM CHOMSKY

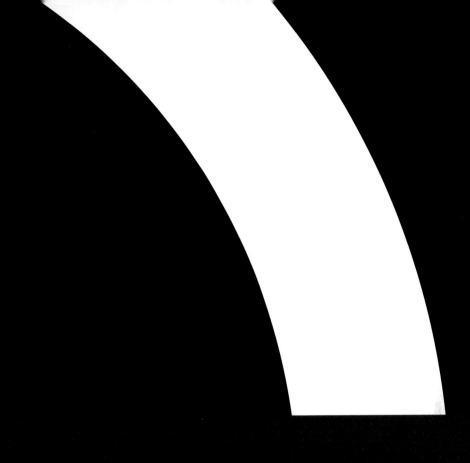

Only two organisations ever formally adopted Holtom's icon as their 'official'
emblem: the Campaign for Nuclear Disarmament and the Greek Committee
of 100. Holtom's symbol actually represented CND; the sign appeared on all
its literature, leaflets and banners, and most of CND's supporters wore it as
a badge. The annual march from Aldermaston to London, winding its way
through the countryside, looked like a medieval army with its pennants and
lollipop signs, and the great banners at the front and rear announcing the
destination and purpose, all in the same stark black-and-white livery with
sans-serif lettering. And central to CND's stark graphics was Holtom's icon.
By the early 1960s most people in Britain were familiar with it and knew that
it meant 'Ban the Bomb!'

An Easter pilgrimage

The first Aldermaston march began on a sunny day, although the BBC said it was the coldest Good Friday in London for years. A crowd of 10,000 people listened to speeches in Trafalgar Square, before 4,000 started the march that stopped at the Albert Memorial in Hyde Park. Then the hard-core demonstrators left for Aldermaston. It was easy to see who was walking the whole way; they were the ones with walking boots, windbreakers, and backpacks – though some came unprepared. The march was impressive, with 700 people chanting slogans and singing campaign songs. The first day ended at Turnham Green.

The next day, however, was difficult. The destination was Slough, it was bitterly cold, and morning snow had turned to rain. 'The coldest holiday Saturday this century, and already it is the wettest Easter holiday since 1900', reported the BBC. The demonstrators marched down the dreary Great West Road, through open countryside, soaking wet, being splashed by passing cars, singing the lyrics to popular songs and chanting slogans if anyone was near enough to hear. Along the way, they distributed leaflets, countered the taunts of pedestrians, or stopped to explain the cause to the curious. Occasionally they received new marchers into their ranks.

FOR THE CHILDREN

Many of the onlookers were moved to see so many children in pushchairs – clearly the best way to travel – which brought home forcefully the reason people were marching. It was hard to heap abuse on parents who sincerely believed that their child's future was threatened. And bobbing above their heads were the lollipop nuclear disarmament signs that would come to characterise the campaign and later on become a symbol for peace itself. The rain turned once more to snow, the first Easter snow for a century. At the Peggy Bedford Inn in Canfield, the landlord was sympathetic and distributed free soup to keep the marchers going. A head count

showed only 300 people; the 'celebrities' hadn't realised that they were expected to march the whole way and Frank Allaun was the only Member of Parliament there, although according to *Peace News*, the numbers never fell below 540. When they reached Slough, a Methodist minister opened his church for them and, with only an hour's notice, somehow managed to produce tea and biscuits for everyone. Shoes were soaked through, causing blisters, and many people without rainwear were soaked to the skin. Blistered feet and swollen ankles were treated by a St John's ambulance team. By now the march consisted mostly of hardy young people, idealists determined to see it through.

CELEBRITIES

On Sunday the march reached Reading, and by Easter Monday VIPs such as literary critic Kenneth Tynan, the writer, Doris Lessing, poet, Christopher Logue and Canon Collins had appeared once more. A head count now revealed 4,000 people trudging their way along the country lanes southwest to Aldermaston. Author Mervyn Jones, remembering this first march, wrote: 'None of us had seen the place where the bombs were made, and we peered at it with a sense of awe as we marched along the perimeter fence. Mysterious pipes led in all directions; the buildings were sinister just

The presence of many children on the Aldermaston marches implied to the public at large – via evocative news pictures such as this – what the CND was all about.

This rally in Trafalgar Square preceded the 1958 march, which was from London to Aldermaston. In subsequent years the march would go in the other direction, climaxing in the square on Easter Monday.

because of their apparent attractiveness and innocence … . At a crossroads we were joined by a healthy contingent from Wessex. Looking back from a hill, we saw the column stretching as far as the road was visible. Friends shouted to each other in delight; cameras clicked. After the doubts, after the crossed fingers, our venture was a success. We had truly started something.'

A CHANGE OF DIRECTION

It was immediately obvious to the organisers that the march was going in the wrong direction. The original idea had been to spark interest in the campaign among the workers at the atomic bomb factory, and only a few people were expected to march; now there was a national campaign and the march had become its centrepiece. Clearly, the march needed to finish in London, where the public and the media were, and so the next year, 1959, the order reversed and it began at the Atomic Weapons Establishment.

By now the Campaign for Nuclear Disarmament had taken over the organisation, and a couple of months after the first march, its members asked Gerald Holtom if they could adopt his nuclear disarmament design as the official CND symbol. Of course, he agreed, but it was decided that the design would not be copyrighted. CND states on its website: 'Although specifically designed for the anti-nuclear movement, it has quite deliberately never been copyrighted. No one has to pay or to seek permission before they use it. A symbol of freedom, it is free for all. This, of course, sometimes leads to its use, or misuse, in circumstances that CND and the peace movement find distasteful. It is also often exploited for commercial, advertising or fashion purposes. We can't stop this happening, and have no intention of copyrighting it. All we can do is to ask commercial users if they would like to make a donation. Any money received is used for CND's peace education and information work.'

Later that summer around 30 members of the DAC, including Pat Arrowsmith, journeyed to

Impromptu jazz bands
were always included
on the marches, as were
folk singers, brass bands
and even a classical
string quartet that
serenaded marchers
from the pavement as
they passed.

Aldermaston once more and demanded to see the director of the site to present their views to him personally. He declined, and so the 30 members declared that they would stay at the site, on the open-access car park forecourt, until the director met with them.

For seven days and nights the protestors camped at the site, with no tents and too few sleeping bags to distribute, attracting local attention and with police in constant attendance. At the end of the week, Lord Soper, a socialist and pacifist minister, was led onto the forecourt by Arrowsmith, with newsmen in tow. The site director finally gave in and agreed to meet them.

THE SECOND YEAR

In 1959, on the basis of the attendance the previous year, CND organisers expected about 700 people to gather at Falcon Field, outside the weapons establishment, to march to London. On Good Friday some 4,300 people waited for the march to begin, with banners and lollipops ready. The baggage vans drove off, the banners were positioned and the marchers began the 53-mile (85.2-k) trek to Trafalgar Square led by Canon Collins and various dignitaries, followed by Holtom's huge march banner with the 'from' and 'to' now reversed to read 'March to London from Aldermaston', but with a fresh bunch of daffodils on top. Several other countries had representatives on the 1959 march: sponsored groups from Germany, Sweden and France walked with their banners, and Australians, Spanish, Norwegian, Irish, Iraqi, Cypriot, Belgian, Danish, Venezuelan, American and Tanganyikan nationals walked with their country's banners. The march had taken on an international aspect.

It was a formidable task to organise a long march such as this, with stopovers, toilets, refreshments and sleeping arrangements, particularly as the organisers had no real idea of how many people would attend. In the following years, for a long time, early on Good Friday, organising secretary Peggy Duff and her

The second Aldermaston march streams through the Berkshire countryside, its head banner amended to mark the reversal of the route.

MARCH
LONDON
FROM
ALDERMASTON
FOOD OR
buy milk
on the march
EXETER
COLLEGE
Oxford

Bookmark for

LEFT, LEFT, LEFT
A personal account of six protest campaigns 1945-65
by PEGGY DUFF
published by Allison & Busby £2.80

A personal account of six protest campaigns 1945-65

team would gather in Falcon Field, across the road from the gates to the AWRE. There would be some early marchers and people who camped overnight in tents, exchanging greetings and preparing for the day. The mobile toilet team arrived early to open their tents on the edge of the field and near the Falcon Inn. Next came the police, then the 7-ton trucks to carry the baggage; first 6, next 8, 10 and then 12, with more added each year as the march grew in size. They were parked in a row, surrounded by duffel bags, sleeping bags, piles of blankets, and labelled knapsacks; each truck had a coloured label, with luggage colour coded to match its transport. The trucks delivered the baggage to the school or hall where the marchers were sleeping and the system usually worked well. Then the buses hired by local groups would begin to arrive from all over Britain.

'A MOVING SIGHT'

Peggy Duff, in *Left, Left, Left,* described the immense sight of the march moving off: 'Then out with the catering vans and all other transport that had to get away before the march. Up to the gate with the Co-op van. Raise the head banner with its bunch of daffodils. Call up the head party and off we went. In front the TV cars with their cameras precariously perched on top. Next to them the Alberts, complete with trombone and whippet. Then the head banner, and behind it, mile after mile, the Aldermaston march.'

The Alberts, a strange surrealist Edwardian 1920s-style jazz band, traditionally led the march in the early years. Then followed approximately 15,000 people, marching along empty country lanes. Behind the people came banner vans, medical teams, marshals' vans, transport for stragglers and children and finally the litter team.

In 1961, the Aldermaston to London march was led by the future leader of the British Labour Party, Michael Foot (with walking stick).

BERTRAND RUSSELL

The philosopher, historian and mathematician Bertrand Russell, 3rd Earl Russell, was born on 18 May 1872, and died at the age of 97 on 2 February 1970. One of the world's best-known intellectuals, in 1950, he received a Nobel Laureate in Literature 'in recognition of his varied and significant writings in which he champions humanitarian ideals and freedom of thought'. Throughout his life he engaged with the events of the day: women's suffrage, birth control, free love, free trade, communism, ethics, atheism, antiwar activities in both world wars, antinuclear activism and opposition to the war in Vietnam.

In 1916, during the Great War, Russell was dismissed from Trinity College, Cambridge, for his pacifist activities and served six months in Brixton jail during which time he wrote *Introduction to Mathematical Philosophy*, his last significant work on mathematics and logic. His magisterial three-volume, *Principia Mathematica*, had been published between 1910 and 1913. He spent an hour talking with Lenin in Moscow in 1920 but was disillusioned by the Soviet system – he regarded himself as a socialist, not a communist. In 1940, he joined the staff of City College in New York, but a public outcry that the author of *Marriage and Morals* (1930) was

'morally unfit' to teach meant that his appointment was rescinded by the court.

Russell was also an atheist and believed that systematic ideologies – all religions and idealogical beliefs such as communism – act to impede knowledge and are responsible for almost all the oppression, misery and warfare in the world. He summed up his lifelong opposition to warmongering with the aphorism: 'War does not determine who is right, only who is left.'

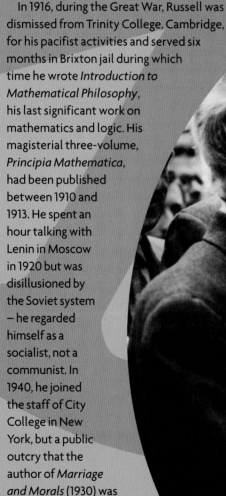

Bertrand Russell with his wife outside London's Bow Street Magistrate's Court, where the 89-year-old philosopher was accused of 'inciting members of the public to commit breaches of the peace' in September 1961.

Pat Arrowsmith, the Committee of 100 activist and leading advocate of nonviolent civil disobedience, wrote *Jericho* – a novel set in the British peace movement of the late 1950s – in 1964, while serving a sentence at Holloway women's prison, London. Herb Greer's, *Mud Pie*, was a then definitive history of the CND, with detailed accounts of the birth of the peace sign. The book was published in London in 1964.

SLEEPING ARRANGEMENTS

Many were inexperienced walkers and, by the time they arrived at each day's destination, they were wet, tired and hungry, and many had blisters. The organisers pointed them towards the hall or school they would sleep in. Some partied, but most collapsed with exhaustion. In 1962 and 1963 the marchers slept beneath canvas in King's Meadows at Reading. In latter years there was a huge marquee that housed 2,000 people. In Slough and other towns, sympathetic councils opened town and village halls, and on one occasion in Slough, the Council Chamber itself.

A NEW DESIGN

After designing the initial symbol and templates for banners, Holtom seems to have dropped out of the movement. None of the other campaign organisers knew him well, and it is as if he gave all he could to the movement by designing the peace symbol, then took his leave. Designer, Ken Garland, took over the designs for the 1962 march. First he was approached by Robin Fior from the Committee of 100 splinter group to design a poster for use on the London Underground. There had been a split within CND between supporters of Canon Collins, who believed in changing UK defence policy by working in the Labour Party and parliament to influence opinion, and followers of Bertrand Russell's stance, prepared to break the law and go to jail to highlight the danger of nuclear war.

The Committee of 100 organised many smaller demonstrations, often ending in sit-ins at which everyone was arrested, including Russell himself. The two factions were still in close contact and after seeing Garland's Committee of 100 poster, Peggy Duff told him: 'I want you to work for us and I would like you also to get some other designers together to work for us.'

'There was never a good war or a bad peace.'

— BENJAMIN FRANKLIN

'Peggy turned up one Sunday morning and said, "We need a poster for showing in the Tube next week"', Garland remembers. 'So I took the existing poster and gradually laid one poster on top of another and felt it said something about a march — like the dawn of something, like when the moon comes to full size from being small crescents.' Even when just a fragment of Holtom's symbol was visible, it was still immediately recognisable. Designers loved its versatility. The only restriction, early on, was that they stick to Holtom's original request that it remain strictly black and white.

It was Garland who designed the tall banners used on the 1963 Easter march: 'We had issued each CND branch with stencils and cheap black cloth so that they could make their own banners containing slogans such as "[name of their town] Against H Bases". When the banners came together on the day, they looked as though they had all been done by one hand. On the march I could not believe it. There were so many hundreds of them, and when we marched along Whitehall, it looked like an invading army. I got a letter from the chairman of CND, Canon Collins, saying that the banners were "quite the most efficient and attractive we have ever had". Some time later, though, I felt a little queasy about them — they reminded me of the long banners used so effectively at Nazi rallies.'

A COMMON HUMANITY

A long-lasting aspect of the marches was the friendships made and the tremendous amount of learning that occurred. Often you would see an older figure surrounded by a group of young people conducting an impromptu seminar on politics, culture, or avant garde art as they walked. Poets met other poets, and musicians formed pick-up bands. One monk dragged a huge cross along the entire route, and there was a group of Buddhist monks, marching without banners, heads bowed in silent meditation.

The chief constable of Berkshire allowed pubs lining the route to remain open to furnish toilet facilities, with publicans doing more business in a few hours than they did in a month: People sat under tables and on top of the piano, jammed the corridors, and filled the pavement outside, all clutching their pints.

Doris Lessing wrote about the first march in *Walking in the Shade*: 'The most heartbreaking and delightful of all the banners was the little one fixed on top of a frail pushchair propelled by a pretty young woman, a brave amateur effort, low down among the great union banners, Labour Party banners, CND banners: "Clydeside says NO" ... "Cornwall says NO" ... "Greenwich says NO" ... "Ban the Bomb" ... all in black on white, but hers said: "Caroline says NO". If I were to choose one image that summed up the years of marches, it would be that one.'

Designer Ken Garland's banners, which he produced for the 1963 Aldermaston gathering, made a spectacular display as the march passed by the daunting towers of Windsor Castle.

FROM ALDERMASTON
TO UNITED NATIONS
VIA LONDON

平
和

PATIENTS OF "A"
SEND THEIR
THE HIROSHIMA
PEACE

Survivors of the
Hiroshima bomb were
among those taking
part in the 1962
Aldermaston march.

COMMITTEE OF 100

◄ Lord and Lady Russell leading the first Committee of 100 demonstration, flanked by (left) the Rev. Michael Scott and (right) American activist, Ralph Schoenman. In the left foreground is Michael Randle, Committee of 100 organiser.

In 1960, Bertrand Russell resigned his presidency of the Campaign for Nuclear Disarmament after a series of confrontations with CND chairman Canon Collins over the direction the campaign was going. Collins believed that the way to achieve their aims was to influence a sufficient number of Labour Party MPs as to make nuclear disarmament Labour Party policy. Russell thought that the threat to humanity was too great to take the slow route of changing the mind of the political establishment.

In the *New Statesman*, February, 1961, Russell wrote: 'If all those who disapprove of government policy were to join massive demonstrations of civil disobedience they could render government folly impossible, and compel the so-called statesmen to acquiesce in measures that would make human survival possible.' There were 108 original Committee of 100 signatories, including writers John Braine, Herbert Read, Alex Comfort, Shelagh Delaney, Christopher Logue, John Osborne and Arnold Wesker; artists such as Augustus John; singer, George Melly; filmmaker, Lindsay Anderson; theatre director, Sir Bernard Miles, and many political activists.

The Committee of 100's first act of civil disobedience was in February 1961 when 5,000 activists staged a sit-in outside the War Office in Whitehall, London. This was followed by demonstrations outside the embassies of the USA and USSR, marches and further sit-ins including blocking the roads at the Polaris submarine base in Holy Loch, Scotland. Thirty-six of the most active demonstrators were

▶ Committee of 100 activist and organiser, Michael Randle, is greeted outside London's Wormwood Scrubs prison in 1963 after serving time for direct-action offences.

summoned to court on 12 September charged with 'inciting members of the public to commit breaches of the peace'. As a way of preventing further demonstrations, they were asked to bind themselves to a promise of good behaviour for twelve months or face a one-month prison sentence. Thirty-two chose to go to jail for their principles.

On 12 September there was a massive demonstration in Trafalgar Square at which Bertrand Russell was arrested during a particularly violent police action which contrasted strongly with the non-violence of the demonstrators. The decision to jail the 89-year-old Russell for a week made headlines around the world, drawing attention to the peace cause, but ultimately the Committee of 100 received less public support than expected and it disbanded in 1968.

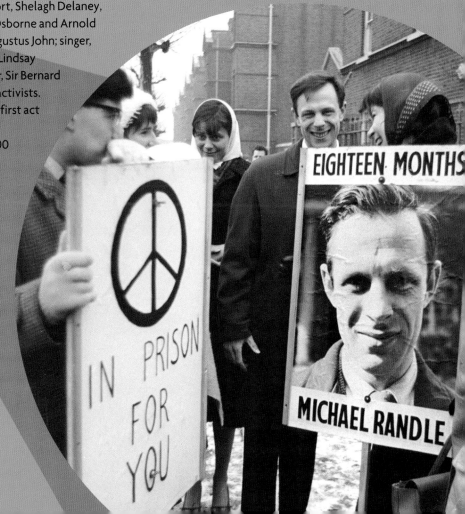

PEACE AROUND
THE WORLD

Following the international media attention paid to the Aldermaston marches and Committee of 100 actions, it didn't take long for the peace symbol to be recognised, and used, around the world. The first instance of its appearance in the USA was via pacifist Bayard Rustin, who helped organise the Committee for Non-Violent Action and Civil Rights March on Washington in 1963. And that same year, the only body to formally adopt the symbol, the Greek Committee of 100, had its confrontation with the government authorities, which led to the infamous death of activist Gregory Lambrakis. But it was with the USA's increasing military involvement in Vietnam and the simultaneous emergence of the youth-led counterculture that a universal call for peace resonated around the planet.

A global message

The peace symbol reached the USA within a few weeks of its being designed, thanks to American pacifist, Bayard Rustin, who had made the trip from the USA to take part in the first Aldermaston march as a representative of the War Resisters League (WRL). From 1947 until 1953, under the aegis of the Fellowship of Reconciliation (FOR), Rustin travelled throughout India, then on to Africa to study the nonviolent aspects of the Indian and Ghanaian independence movements.

The FOR was originally started in 1914 in an attempt to prevent the spread of war in Europe and went on to encourage conscientious objectors to refuse to serve in World War II, in Vietnam and in subsequent wars. In 1953 Rustin became executive secretary of the War Resisters League, a post he held for 12 years. (It was during this time that he was arrested for refusing to take part in the civil defence drill in New York City.)

On leave from the WRL, in 1956 he was an adviser to Dr Martin Luther King, Jr, on how to apply Gandhian principles of nonviolence to the boycott of public transportation then taking shape in Montgomery, Alabama. He also played an important role in the birth of the Southern Christian Leadership Conference, and in the Prayer Pilgrimage to Washington that took place on 17 May 1957, to urge President Eisenhower to enforce the Supreme Court's 1954 ruling that the nation's schools should be desegregated.

'I HAVE A DREAM'
The high point of Bayard Rustin's career was without doubt his role as the chief organiser of the March on Washington for Jobs and Freedom held on 28 August 1963, when Dr King delivered his stirring 'I Have a Dream' speech. After the first Aldermaston march, Bayard Rustin returned to the USA, taking posters and peace-symbol badges with him, and so it was through him that by the summer of 1958, the symbol was being used by both antiwar and antinuclear groups, as well as by the growing civil rights movement with which he was actively involved.

VOYAGE OF THE *GOLDEN RULE*
It was probably through Rustin, a fellow Quaker and pacifist activist, that Albert Bigelow was introduced to the symbol. Bigelow was one of 12 members of the Committee for Non-Violent Action (CNVA) formed in 1957, and arrested that same year for attempting to enter the Camp Mercury nuclear test site in Nevada. He had been involved in the American Friends Service Committee, a Quaker organisation that raised a petition calling for an end to atmospheric nuclear tests, and he was a committed activist.

Bigelow was a former American navy commander, and in February 1958 he and his crew of four set sail in the 30-foot (9-m) ketch *Golden Rule* to enter the Pentagon's atmospheric test site at the Eniwetok atoll proving grounds in the Marshall Islands. The Atomic Energy Commission quickly made it illegal to enter the test area, and when *Golden Rule* set sail from Hawaii, they were intercepted and arrested, even though they were only five nautical miles from Honolulu. They tried again on 4 June, but this time they were arrested, charged with contempt of court, and given 60 days in jail. Albert Bigelow wrote: 'When you see something horrible happening, your instinct is to do something about it. You can

The 6 September 1963, edition of *Life* magazine featured the civil rights March on Washington for Jobs and Freedom – also known as the Freedom March – organised by A. Philip Randolph (left) and Bayard Rustin.

LIFE

Another Sacrifice by Fire
FLAMES OF FURY IN VIETNAM

HOLLYWOOD'S GREAT ENIGMA,
BURT LANCASTER

In Color:
SPECTACLE
of the
MARCH

NEW
YORK
EXTRA
SECTION

THE LEADERS:
RANDOLPH
AND RUSTIN

American activists.
Bayard Rustin (left)
and Marvin Gewirtz
(next to him) join a
group of American
protesters about to
leave for the Soviet
Union to protest against
Russian (and also British)
nuclear tests in 1958.
This nonviolent action
group also sponsored
the *Golden Rule* to
sail into the forbidden
American nuclear test
zone in the Pacific.

▶ Albert S. Bigelow was captain of *Golden Rule* and leader of the Quaker direct-action group attempting to sail into the nuclear test zone.

◀ The *Golden Rule* protest ship with its crew of five in February 1958, about to set sail from Hawaii for the American atomic test site on the Eniwetok atoll in the South Pacific.

freeze in fearful apathy or you can even talk yourself into saying that it isn't horrible. I can't do that. I have to act. This is too horrible. We know it. Let's all act.'

WORLDWIDE EXPOSURE

During their widely publicised attempts to interrupt the nuclear test, the newly created unilateral nuclear-disarmament flag fluttered from the ship's mast, thus spreading the peace symbol around the world. The Committee for Non-Violent Action continued to use the symbol on some of its publicity and this tradition lives on with the War Resisters League, the pacifist organisation that the CNVA merged with in 1968 after the death of their inspirational leader, A. J. Muste.

Although none of the American organisations adopted the peace symbol officially in the way that the CND had done, it was used as a convenient shorthand symbol for peace by many groups at the time.

'You can't separate peace from freedom because no one can be at peace unless he has his freedom.'

– MALCOLM X

BEAT PEACE

There was another early American connection to the peace symbol. In May 1958, about a month after the first Aldermaston march, American Beat Generation poets, Allen Ginsberg and Gregory Corso, visited Britain from Paris, where they were both living at the so-called Beat Hotel on the Left Bank. At a poetry reading at New College, Oxford, they found themselves in the middle of a controversy: Corso's lighthearted approach to the subject of the H-Bomb in his new poem 'Bomb' was regarded as outrageous: 'O Bomb I love you/ I want to kiss your clank, eat your boom … '.

New College was the main CND stronghold in Oxford. Led by Steven Hugh-Jones, the editor of *Isis*, the members of the New College Poetry Society showed their feelings by removing their shoes and throwing them at Corso, calling him a fascist. Ginsberg reported to his boyfriend Peter Orlovsky: 'The students got mad and attacked him for being, they thought, antisocial. "Do you know what it's like to die by an H-Bomb?" they

yelled.' Corso was offended and called them a bunch of creeps. After a brief argument, Ginsberg called them assholes and the reading ended in disharmony. Matters improved at the party afterwards, though. 'Big funny time', Ginsberg wrote to Orlovsky. Back in London, Ginsberg helped to distribute CND leaflets, then returned to Paris with leaflets and a big bag of badges, some of which accompanied him back to New York a few months later.

The peace symbol reached its widest audience yet in 1960 when Philip Altbach, a student at the University of Chicago, went to London as a delegate of the Student Peace Union (SPU). Philip Altbach remembered:

I was in the UK to speak to the national Campaign for Nuclear Disarmament and was impressed by their symbol – the peace symbol – and I put a few of the buttons and little flags in my pocket and brought them back to SPU headquarters in Chicago. I managed to convince (there was some reluctance) the SPU officers to let us print up 20,000 buttons as a

Poet, Allen Ginsberg – a tireless campaigner for peace in the 1960s – takes time out while filming the 1959 experimental movie, *Pull My Daisy*, resting across fellow 'beats' Peter Orlovsky (left) and Gregory Corso.

THE SATAN SELLER

The idea that the peace symbol without its circle once signified the devil, or is an insult to Christianity, is a myth propagated by Mike Warnke, whose 1972 book *The Satan Seller* has sold over 3 million copies in 20 years and is used by many law-enforcement agencies in the USA when dealing with so-called 'occult' crime. The Christian magazine *Cornerstone* wrote: 'We believe that *The Satan Seller* has been responsible, more than any other single volume in the Christian market, for promoting the current nationwide "Satanism scare". The magazine investigated Warnke and found that the entire book was bogus. He claimed to have been the leader of a coven of 1,500

satanists, to have been a long-haired hippie involved in high-level drug deals, and even to have two 'love slaves' available to obey his every command. *Cornerstone*'s thorough investigation found out that his girlfriend at the time would not even let him drink and would certainly not have sex with him, being a devout Catholic. Photographs in his pre-minister days show him as short-haired and respectable.

Cornerstone interviewed friends and teachers and found it was all fantasy; at the most, he may have had an illicit beer with friends. But his claim to have put Satan behind him and converted to Christianity enabled him to set himself up as a minister. He quickly became a millionaire.

He became known as 'America's number one Christian Comedian'. His records sold in the millions, he appeared on the Oprah Winfrey and Larry King shows, and 29 June 1988, was declared Mike Warnke Day by the governor of Tennessee – all on the strength of his renouncing a satanic background that was complete fiction.

In his book Warnke quotes some of his born-again friends: 'We got rid of our peace symbols after we got saved', Sue said, 'because we found out it had a satanic origin ... It was used on Hitler's Nazi death notices and as part of the official inscription on gravestones of Nazi officers of the SS, the leaders of which ... were Satanists ....'

Warnke also claims that the peace symbol was a favourite sign of Satanists in both the Middle Ages and the present day, in Austria and Italy meaning evil and death. Then he states the theory of Nero's cross, that St Peter asked to be crucified upside down because he was not worthy to die in the same manner as

Part of the cover illustration for the infamous 'satanism scare' exposé, *The Satan Seller* (1972), by Mike Warnke, which proved to be little more than an elaborate, but profitable, hoax.

THE SATAN SELLER

MIKE WARNKE
WITH DAVE BALSIGER AND LES JONES

A print by the Dutch artist and Anabaptist pastor, Jan Luyken (1649–1712), of the 'upside down' crucifixion of St Peter, published in an 1865 edition of *Martyrs Mirror*.

Jesus. 'Nero is said to have granted the request and constructed the cross like the peace symbol. Since that time, it has been known as the symbol of the antichrist, and in AD 70 it was the signet carried by the Romans who ravished Jerusalem.'

Gerry O'Sullivan at the University of Pennsylvania wrote in *Delusion: The Satanism Scare* (1991): 'Hundreds of professional training manuals on satanism and "occult-related crime" have appeared over the past several years, aimed at police officers, pastors, school administrators and psychologists ... Based upon

incorrect information in such training manuals, schools in Kentucky, Florida and California – among others – have banned the wearing of peace symbols on T-shirts or in jewellery because it is, in reality, the satanic "cross of Nero" ... This is an old right-wing canard ... later picked up and circulated by "former satanic high priest", Mike Warnke, in a wildly popular little anti-occult book called *The Satan Seller*. Unfortunately, this piece of folklore has appeared and reappeared in police guides over the years.'

'I think that people want peace so much that one of these days governments had better get out of the way and let them have it.'

— DWIGHT D. EISENHOWER

first try. We distributed them to our chapters, sold them at meetings, and 'the rest is history'. My guess is that SPU probably printed at least 100,000 little pins. The Committee for Nonviolent Action in Chicago, and probably FOR, used the symbol before SPU, but SPU – which was the largest progressive student organisation in the USA at the time – brought the symbol to wide attention.

PRONUCLEAR BACKLASH

Predictably, efforts were attempted to discredit the nuclear disarmament movement and the antiwar lobby from the beginning; in Britain none of the major newspapers gave them impartial coverage, always downplaying the attendance at rallies, focusing on the few eccentric people present on a march, or running lengthy rebuttals from pronuclear factions. In the USA with its large conservative Bible Belt, more unorthodox

While some Christian groups in the USA associated the peace sign with devil worship and worse, others were totally sympathetic, such as Bishop James A. Pike of San Francisco, who pledged to wear his peace symbol medallion 'until we cease our invasion of Vietnam'.

tactics were used, and an extraordinary attempt was made to discredit the peace symbol itself. One particular piece of disinformation, widely promoted by the far-right John Birch Society and believed by many even now, was to claim that the symbol was really a disguised version of the 'broken cross', apparently a sign of the Antichrist. According to the Birchites, this form of cross had been devised by the Roman emperor Nero, who had St Peter crucified on it, nailed upside-down. Because of this, they claimed that in the Middle Ages the symbol was used to signify the devil. Accordingly, the John Birch Society accused the peace movement of repudiating Christ.

It is probably true that St Peter was crucified upside-down – the apocryphal Acts of Peter, for instance, describes Peter as having been crucified upside down. Although the same text has Peter resurrecting smoked fish and causing dogs to

Greek peace activist, Gregory Lambrakis (left), with Bayard Rustin (centre) at the Oxford Peace Conference in January 1963.

ATHENS

One of the few other peace groups in the world to formally adopt the peace sign was the Greek Committee of 100, based in Athens. In 1963, a Marathon to Athens peace march was planned, organised by a Greek division of Bertrand Russell's Committee of 100 set up by Michael Peristerakis, a law student, from Athens. They were opposed to nuclear bases on Greek soil and to American Polaris submarines being based in Greek ports. A Greek Peace Committee was already in existence, but it was basically a wing of the EDA party and like most 'peace committees', it was heavily influenced, and probably financed, by the Soviet Union (just as most 'freedom' organisations were CIA funded). Peristerakis was nonaligned and wanted the Greek Committee of 100 to be similarly independent.

A small British contingent arrived in Athens 12 days before the march, and to their surprise they were immediately taken to a press conference. In the following days they were entertained with the greatest hospitality, and everywhere they were applauded. Bertrand Russell appeared to be the most popular Englishman in Athens. Then three days before the march, one of the English contingent, John Petherbridge, was arrested and taken to Athens police headquarters, where he was fingerprinted and photographed. Four hours later he was released, only to be arrested again two days later, along with the other members of his party. He was forcibly searched and questioned about the march because, although the Greek Constitution guaranteed the right to demonstrate, the right-wing government had banned the march. When he refused to answer questions, he was told: 'We have ways of making you talk.' He laughed it off, not realising that they were serious.

Then the head interrogator entered the room, the blinds were drawn, and Petherbridge's glasses were removed. 'The new arrival slapped me hard across the face and then departed without saying anything', Petherbridge wrote. 'My glasses were returned, and I was put in a bare cell. To pass the time, I scratched a large CND symbol on the wall.'

Petherbridge and the others were deported, and other British supporters were arrested and deported as they arrived by train. Anyone wearing the peace sign was turned back at the frontiers and airports.

Pat Arrowsmith, on a tourist visit to the Oracle at Delphi, was denied access because of her CND badge, which was confiscated. She and her companion that day returned to Athens, then reported the affront and decided that more of them should return the following day all wearing their badges. Pat made a new one using paper and pen. The next day, fearing adverse publicity with numerous news cameramen following Pat and her coach party, the Oracle was declared open to them. However, she and her friends were followed around by Greek secret policemen who were not so secret in their work. On spotting them, Pat decided to follow her trackers, which somewhat confused the policemen. On leaving the Oracle, the CND contingent visited a bar and ordered retsina – for the secret policemen as well as themselves. Disconcerted, the drinks were refused, much to Pat's amusement. It was to prove a rare moment of levity during the visit.

GREGORY LAMBRAKIS

On Easter Sunday 10,000 police were mobilised to stop the march and more than 1,000 people were arrested for trying to get through their cordons. Only one man managed to walk the full distance, Gregory Lambrakis, who, as an independent member of the Greek Parliament, was immune from arrest. Lambrakis had attended the Oxford CND conference in January 1963, and he walked the 2.5 km (4 miles) from Marathon to Athens bearing the same banner, reading ELLAS, that he carried when he marched the full distance on that year's Aldermaston march. He had adopted the CND sign for the Greek peace movement.

A CND demonstration in London protested the murder of Gregory Lambrakis. The floral wreath in the shape of the peace sign was placed outside the railings of Buckingham Palace, where the king and queen of Greece were due to visit two days later.

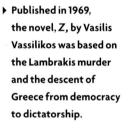

▶ Published in 1969,
the novel, Z, by Vasilis
Vassilikos was based on
the Lambrakis murder
and the descent of
Greece from democracy
to dictatorship.

◀ Two young women
wearing CND badges
and displaying the
journal of the Young
Communist League,
Challenge, protest at
the arrival in Britain of
King Paul and Queen
Frederika of Greece in
July 1963 after the
murder of the Greek
peace campaigner,
Gregory Lambrakis.

Four weeks later, as he finished addressing
a meeting of his constituents in Salonica, the
hall he was in was surrounded by members of a
fascist group. He appealled for police protection,
but it was refused. When he attempted to leave,
he was deliberately run over by a motorcycle and
sidecar; he died from his injuries.

It was a political assassination, and half a
million people brought Athens to a standstill for
his funeral. 'Throughout the morning, groups of
people made their way to the cathedral carrying
enormous flowered wreaths made up in the
CND symbol', wrote David Boulton in the CND
weekly, *Sanity*. 'During the funeral procession
itself, flowers and symbol wreaths were flung
into the streets from the houses and shops along

the route. Behind the coffin walked a dozen members or so of the Athens Committee of 100, carrying a plain silk banner decorated with the symbol.' Lambrakis's grave is marked by a plain grey stone into which the peace symbol has been carved. The story of Lambrakis was the basis for Vasilis Vassilikos's novel, *Z*, and its subsequent film by Costa-Gavras in 1970. Lambrakis's assassin was finally brought to justice, but not until after several witnesses 'died in mysterious circumstances'.

STATE VISIT

The repressive Greek regime hoped to gain some respectability with a state visit by Queen Frederika and King Paul to Britain that July, but the threat of demonstrations on the London streets led the Greek prime minister, Karamanlis, to recommend that the visit be postponed. He was overruled and resigned his post in protest. Two days before the Greek royal family arrived, CND held a march down Piccadilly in memory of Gregory Lambrakis and left a floral wreath in the shape of the peace symbol at the railings in front of Buckingham Palace, where it was immediately removed by a small man wearing a bowler hat who took it inside the palace.

On 11 July, during the state visit, to show support for the Greek peace movement, the Committee of 100 held a demonstration with banners headed 'Against Tyranny'.

It was at the trials of people arrested at this demonstration that the police were found to have 'planted' halfhouse-bricks on eight of the defendants. There was no trace of brick dust in the defendants' pockets, and the house bricks were found to conveniently fit together. In the resulting trial the arresting officer, Det. Sgt. Harold Challenor, was found to be insane: He had long wanted to be the first policeman on the moon and walked 20 miles (32 km) to work to get in training. As a result of the Challenor Affair, dozens of previous convictions were quashed and numerous people had to be

Two American demonstrators prepare to spend the night in New York's Times Square during a 1961 peace protest.

released from jail, having been found guilty on falsified evidence. In March 1964, Challenor and three of his fellow officers were charged with conspiracy to prevent the course of justice. Challenor was sent for treatment for paranoid schizophrenia, and the other three received three years each.

HIGH SCHOOL PROTEST

As American intervention in Vietnam and Southeast Asia increased, the use of the peace sign proliferated across the USA. Although the press tried to marginalise peace protesters as being lefties or hippies, opposition to the war in Vietnam came from people in all walks of life. Nor was antiwar activity confined to the campuses and crash pads: In one celebrated case, five students at North High School in Des Moines, Iowa, took their case to the Supreme Court after they were suspended from classes for wearing black armbands displaying the peace symbol, which they wore to mourn the Vietnam war dead. On 4 March 1968, two of the children, 13-year-old Mary Beth Tinker (who was in junior high) and her 15-year-old brother John, travelled to Washington, DC, to hear the Supreme Court

debate on how far public schools may go to limit the wearing of political symbols. In the final hearing on 24 February 1969, the court was divided in its opinion and so, accordingly, the previous court decision upholding the school's right to suspend the students was upheld.

The sign appeared on college campuses as well as in hippie neighbourhoods, such as the Lower East Side of New York, Haight-Ashbury in San Francisco, and the Strip in Los Angeles, but it was images taken from this hippie counter-culture and, more particularly, pictures of the Human Be-In, that did much to associate the peace symbol with hippies and the antiwar movement in the USA.

THE HUMAN BE-IN

The Human Be-In, alternatively known as both the Gathering of the Tribes or Pow Wow, was held on 14 January 1967, in the Polo Field of Golden Gate Park, San Francisco. The peace sign was everywhere. People had peace symbols painted on their faces, on their bodies, and on their clothes. Peace was the message of the day. Cutouts of the sign, 46 cm (18 in) across were mounted on long poles and waved high above

Mary Beth Tinker and her brother, John, show the black armbands with peace signs that they wore in protest of the conflict in Vietnam, which led to their and three other students' suspension from their high school in Des Moines, Iowa, in 1968.

'The only thing necessary for the triumph of evil is for good men to do nothing.'

– EDMUND BURKE

A rock fan heads for the now legendary 1969 Woodstock festival in his Ford Mustang, replete with antiwar graffiti.

▲ West Coast hippies at a 'freak-out' in the late 1960s, the peace symbol an inevitable dress item.

◀ Hippies in the Haight-Ashbury district of San Francisco listen to guitar music during the 'summer of love' of 1967.

the heads of the crowd, symbolising the peaceful intention of the gathering. There was no overt political agenda, it was just a friendly picnic and social gathering for 30,000 people. On stage were a group of self-appointed gurus and leaders: Allen Ginsberg, who chanted the *Hari Om Namo Shivaya* mantra to Shiva, 'god' of pot smokers; Timothy Leary, who preached the virtues of LSD ; Gary Snyder, poet of the ecology movement; Lenore Kandel, who read from her *Love Book*; Jerry Rubin, who called for a marriage of the Berkeley politicos and the Haight-Ashbury psychedelic tribes.

People were on acid, distributed free by the Diggers – a radical community-action group, on

pot, or just enjoying the music provided free by the Jefferson Airplane, Moby Grape, the Grateful Dead, Janis Joplin, Big Brother and the Holding Company and many more. At 5:00 P.M. in the afternoon, everyone tidied up the rubbish and went home or made their way to watch the sunset over the Pacific. Allen Ginsberg called it the last great idealistic hippie event.

Later that year, when the weather improved, there were similar events in Central Park, New York, and in the Vondelpark in Amsterdam, where homegrown hippies gathered to hear Dutch psychedelic bands. The miniskirts were shorter, the joints of marijuana larger, the hair longer, and the peace signs – some made from

A rock band performs
at the now legendary
Human Be-In in San
Francisco's Golden Gate
Park, at the height of
'flower power' in
January 1967.

A farmhouse turned
hippie commune in
Meadville, Pennsylvania,
in 1968, emblazoned
with peace signs.

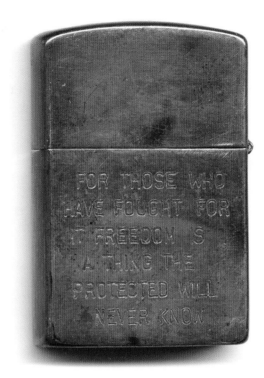

A traditional Zippo cigarette lighter inscribed by troops returning from Vietnam in 1971, with the peace sign and a message: 'For those who have fought for it, freedom is a thing the protected will never know'.

flowers – bigger than anywhere else on Earth. They did not just carry flowers, they carried entire flowering branches. Young people in Amsterdam took the hippie message to heart and made it part of the local culture.

THE DRAFT

One of the reasons the Vietnam war was so unpopular was that young men were being drafted into the armed forces. Many were torn between doing their patriotic duty and opposition to what they saw as an unjust war. The USA had not declared war on North Vietnam and many young people felt that it had no legitimate reason to intervene; indeed, as General Eisenhower himself wrote in his memoirs, if the USA had allowed the people of Vietnam to hold democratic elections, 72 percent would have voted for Ho Chi Minh.

SOLDIERS FOR PEACE

This was not like fighting the Japanese aggressors in World War II, this was the USA imposing a puppet government on a foreign country and many young people did not think that was worth dying for. Families were divided; young men crossed the border to Canada to find sanctuary; others fled to Europe. Because more and more white middle-class kids stayed on at college to get deferment from conscription, a disproportionate number of the troops were Black and Hispanic. Induction centres all across the USA were picketed, some by people carrying American flags with the stars replaced by the peace symbol.

The troops themselves had little of the gung-ho spirit of World War II: They published their own antiwar underground newspapers and painted peace symbols on their helmets. In one celebrated case, when the amphibious warship *Bexar* returned to San Diego, California, on 27 October 1969, some of the 3,000 marines on board draped a large handmade peace symbol over the side of the ship and made peace signs with their fingers for the waiting photographers.

Marines returning home from the Vietnam conflict aboard warship, *Bexar*, in October 1969, make peace signs and display a handmade peace symbol.

The USA shows off its first nuclear surface task force in 1964: aircraft carrier, USS *Enterprise*; missile cruiser, USS *Long Beach* (centre); and the missile frigate, USS *Bainbridge*. Crew personnel on the carrier form Einstein's equation, the basis of the atomic power, which will carry them around the world without refuelling.

CANADA: A VIETNAM DRAFT DODGERS HAVEN

As many as 125,000 American Vietnam War protesters are estimated to have moved north of the border to Canada between 1964 and 1977, approximately 25,000 of whom were young draft-eligible males seeking to avoid mandatory military service. Assisted by Canadian groups, such as the Toronto Anti-Draft Programme, the so-called 'Draft Dodgers' and their fellow American war resisters helped spearhead the antiwar peace effort from the safety of Canadian soil. In 1977, the American president, Jimmy Carter, officially pardoned the Draft Dodgers – as a result of which about half of them then returned home to the USA.

Demonstrators picket for an end to the draft in front of an army induction centre in Los Angeles in 1970.

'Any intelligent fool can make things bigger, more complex, and more violent. It takes a touch of genius – and a lot of courage – to move in the opposite direction.'

– ALBERT EINSTEIN

COUNTERCULTURE

Pictures of Woodstock and other counter-cultural gatherings disseminated the peace symbol across the world, and it quickly became a shorthand, an inexpensive way of suggesting belief in hippie ideals. Children at dress-up parties dressed as hippies by drawing the peace sign on a T-shirt and wearing a headband; students used magic markers to transform an ordinary denim jacket into a statement of teenage rebellion, and, of course, it was a godsend for cartoonists.

But it took courage to wear the peace symbol at the end of the 1960s: American society was so divided over the issue of Vietnam that anyone with long hair or wearing a peace symbol was regarded as the enemy by large sections of society. As these hippie types were largely young people, students, in particular, were singled out by self-proclaimed prowar 'patriots', the police, and the military.

THE KENT STATE SHOOTINGS

This conflict was tragically acted out on 4 May 1970, when students at Kent State University in Ohio demonstrated against President Nixon's decision to invade Cambodia. A contingent of 28 Ohio National Guardsmen were ordered to open fire on the unarmed students. The 13 seconds of fire left 4 students dead, one permanently paralysed, and eight others wounded.

Not every Kent State student was involved in the demonstration; many were simply walking to

This Pulitzer prize-winning photograph by John Filo shows Mary Ann Vecchio kneeling over the body of fellow Kent State student, Jeffrey Miller, after the Ohio National Guard opened fire on an antiwar demonstration, killing four protesters.

and from class. The closest student wounded was 25.5 m (30 yd) away from the Guard, while the farthest was almost 228.5 m (250 yd) away. The incident radicalised students across the land and provoked Neil Young's song 'Ohio', which became a rallying call. Colleges were supposed to be sanctuaries – places of safety where ideas could be explored and debated. That the military could legally occupy a campus and murder unarmed students shocked and horrified large numbers of Americans and stunned the country's student population.

Campuses were occupied by students across the country, many more were closed, classes were disrupted, even at high schools. The polarisation of the country was so bad that the parents of the murdered students not only had to deal with their grief but received large quantities of hate mail about their children, accusing two of them, Allison Krause and Sandra Scheuer, of being 'whores' and all of them of being 'commies'. Yet even at a conservative Catholic college such as Marymount, which was one of the few colleges not to cancel classes, the students demonstrated and carried banners with the ubiquitous peace sign in protest of the deaths on Kent State campus.

Sociologists for Peace demonstrate in Washington, DC, at a protest on behalf of the students killed at Kent State University.

An anti–Vietnam War protester carries a 'Teachers for Peace' pennant and wears a 'Free Angela Davis' T-shirt in a Washington, DC, demonstration for the students killed at Kent State University.

GREENPEACE

One of the most important organisations to stem from the direct-action peace movement is Greenpeace. On 5 August 1971, 20 scientists – activists against nuclear weapons testing – set sail from Vancouver Harbour for Amchitka Island, Alaska, where the USA was scheduled to set off an underground nuclear weapon blast in that October, which was 250 times more powerful than the bomb that had levelled Hiroshima. They were in a rusting fishing trawler named *Greenpeace*, formally the *Phyllis Cormack*, named after the wife of skipper, John Cormack. Their intention was to sail within five miles of the test site, where they would be potentially exposed to radiation and shock waves, in order to protest against the ecological damage that nuclear testing was wreaking on the fragile Arctic ecosystem, and to demonstrate against the proliferation of nuclear weapons and the threat of nuclear war. Also on board were Jim Bohlen, coordinator of the Don't Make Waves Committee, as well as two members of the British Columbia branch of the Sierra Club, Erving Stowe and Paul Cote.

Not unexpectedly, the American Coast Guard quickly arrested ship and crew, but the press and publicity engendered by this action put pressure on the American government, and four months later the USA cancelled the test series. Out of this action came Greenpeace, named after its first ship and first successful action. 'We do not consider ourselves to be radicals', said Ben Metcalfe, one of the activists at the time. 'We are conservatives, who insist upon conserving the environment for our children and future generations of man.'

It was from this relatively humble beginning that the Greenpeace organisation grew. By 2008 Greenpeace has national and regional offices in 42 countries worldwide, all affiliated to Greenpeace International based in Amsterdam. One of Greenpeace's stated aims is to free the world of nuclear weapons. Their plan of action is to get as many countries and cities, states or counties to declare themselves Nuclear Free Zones and thus rid entire parts of the world of nuclear weapons, bit by bit, region by region, shrinking the geographical and political space in which atomic weapons can play a role. More than 50 percent of the world is already in a nuclear weapons free zone, and Greenpeace is working with politicians, unions, religious leaders, doctors, educationalists and others to increase this percentage every day. In November 1980 Manchester was the first local authority in Britain to declare itself a nuclear free zone.

Greenpeace, as described by its official mission statement, ' ... is an independent,

An aerial view shows *Rainbow Warrior*, **the Greenpeace vessel that is still active in the environmental and antiwar movement today. The original** *Rainbow Warrior* **was sunk in Auckland harbour, New Zealand, in July 1985, sabotaged by the French foreign intelligence agency prior to it monitoring French nuclear tests in the Pacific.**

Antinuclear activists in Vancouver in 1971, preparing to set sail with 20 scientists in the *Greenpeace* vessel. The organisation was actually founded in Vancouver earlier that year, with its primary concerns including the environmental issues represented by the whaling industry.

campaigning organisation, which uses peaceful direct action and creative communication to expose global environmental problems and to force solutions for a green and peaceful future. Greenpeace's goal is to ensure the ability of the earth to nurture life in all its diversity.' To do this they always offer an alternative: They campaign against overfishing and advise on marine reserves; they campaign against nuclear energy and for the promotion of renewable energy. And in campaigning against the proliferation of nuclear power stations, they are still closely linked to the original campaign against nuclear weapons.

THE FASHION FOR PEACE

From youth street style to haute couture, as well as in music and films, the peace sign has been a part of popular culture since its inception 50 years ago. As early as the first Aldermaston marches, it became an essential badge for 'beatnik' ban-the-bombers, youngsters whose enthusiasm for jazz and blues evolved into the British rock boom of the 1960s. In the USA, it was adopted by the folk-inspired, protest-rock movement and the late 1960s counterculture that it inspired – although while 'peace 'n' love' was definitely hippie, the peace sign was also appropriated by European punk-anarchists in their

Style icon

The beauty of Holtom's design lies in its simplicity. Anyone can – and many have – reproduced it on innumerable surfaces, in countless materials. It has been worn, carried, spray-painted, stitched, printed, kiln-baked, spun, knitted and constructed across the world since making its debut appearance on the lollipops, badges and banners of 1958. The fact that it was first reproduced on badges that were baked from clay for the original antinuclear march in 1958 was an obvious inspiration for the manufacturers of teenage apparel, both amateur and professional. One didn't need to be a draftsman to create the symbol.

As the gentleman in the derby hat on board the SS *Royal Daffodil* in 1959 (opposite) demonstrates, the peace symbol can make a dramatic fashion statement and marks the wearer as an anti-establishmentarian at first glance. At least, at that size it does. The man on the ship is attending the second Floating Festival of Jazz, featuring British 'trad' (traditional) jazz players such as Chris Barber, sailing from London to the North Sea.

The rest of this man's clothes, from the beard and shapelesss sweater down to his striped knee socks, must have presented a shocking sight in 1958, a time when smartly suited 'Teddy Boys' were considered the height of sartorial inelegance. However, this offered merely a taste of what was to follow in the next decade. The Aldermaston marches of the late 1950s and early 1960s had attracted the impassioned support of idealistic youth who were dying to escape from conformity. While some played traditional jazz and homemade folk music, other English boys were learning to play a half-forgotten music from the Deep South – the blues. On a small island in the Thames, a bunch of blues-obsessed young men would congregate and listen to one another play versions of songs that they had heard on 78-rpm shellac discs. Among them were the members of numerous soon-to-be-famous bands, including the Yardbirds, Cream and The Rolling Stones.

Once the Stones' managers, the ever-enterprising Andrew Loog Oldham and Tony Calder, had decided on the image of bad boys for their charges, the band began to attract fans who were hoping to be seen as anti-Establishment and as rebellious as Jagger, Jones and Richards. With Holtom's symbol folding into British national consciousness as a sign of anti-government direct action and discontent, younger brothers of the 1958 marchers began scratching it into their school desks and inking it onto their jackets.

BEGGAR'S BANQUET

When the Stones chose to depict a toilet wall on the cover of their 1968 album *Beggar's Banquet*, Holtom's symbol sat right underneath the band name, almost in the middle of the cover. The album contains the band's first banned American single, 'Street Fighting Man', as well as 'Sympathy for the Devil', which undoubtedly did more than any other use of Holtom's symbol to spread among the hippie mainstream. The Stones were the first mainstream pop act with number one hit singles on both sides of the Atlantic to become politicised. 'Street Fighting Man' was banned in the greater Chicago area, on release in the autumn of 1968, for inciting a riot (at the time, the Students For a Democratic Society (SDS) and Abbie Hoffman's yippies were staging their biggest demonstration in the city at the

Young British 'ravers' on the traditional jazz scene quickly adopted the CND symbol and made their presence felt at events such as the Floating Festival of Jazz in 1959 and, of course, the Aldermaston march.

Peace-sign sunglasses were sported on the first Italian peace march, which covered 22 km (14 miles) from Perugia to Assisi, in September 1961. The slogan around the lenses reads 'Let's Bury Atom Bombs – Not Humanity'.

'We need, in every community, a group of angelic troublemakers.'

– BAYARD RUSTIN

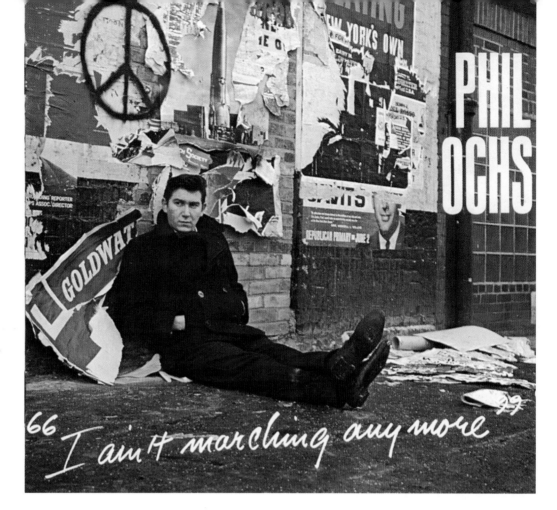

PHIL OCHS

66 *I ain't marching any more* 99

Phil Ochs, one of the major names of the 1960s protest song movement, released the album, *I Ain t Marching Any More*, in 1965, which had a strong antiwar message in its title track as well as a prominent peace sign on the sleeve.

◄ A member of the audience at a 1966 Rolling Stones concert in Paris, France, has 'Remember Hiroshima', drawn graffiti-style on his shirt, above the peace logo (with a Committee of 100 insert).

Democratic convention), which obviously endeared the band to the emerging underground movement in the USA. And while the Beatles were proclaiming that you could count them out of any revolution, the Stones were willing to write the soundtrack for one, or so it seemed, and Holtom's symbol became theirs and, by extension, that of the revolutionary underground hippie culture.

EVE OF DESTRUCTION

It was regrettable, however, that the antinuclear message was being lost. It might not have been if singer/songwriter Barry McGuire had adopted Holtom's symbol for himself. In 1965, he found huge success with the first antinuclear anthem to hit the pop charts. P. F. Sloan's song 'Eve of Destruction' was an international hit for former New Christy Minstrels' member, McGuire. A blatant attempt to ape the success of Bob Dylan (and originally offered to The Byrds, who turned

it down), the song became an American Billboard No. 1 Hit in September 1965 and was immediately castigated by the mainstream press as being the perfect example of everything that was wrong with the younger generation of Americans.

It was adopted by every antiwar and antinuclear movement for a while and proved that a political message could sell pop singles. McGuire became a prominent member of the emerging Hippie A-list and recorded a version of 'California Dreaming' with the Mamas and the Papas in 1966, but never recaptured the level of success that 'Eve of Destruction' had given him. Maybe if he'd also worn the prominent ND badge, he might have endured longer.

But other folk hippies emerged in the wake of McGuire, among them Arlo Guthrie, whose 'Alice's Restaurant Massacre' was a long (in excess of 18 minutes) antiwar song that later became a film in which the singer asks the listener to resist the draft. He harnessed the power of Holtom's

Singer/songwriter Barry
McGuire (shirtless), who
had hit the charts in
1965 with the antiwar
pop anthem 'Eve of
Destruction', joins
fellow musicians at
a 1967 'love-in'.

'The structure of world peace cannot be the work of one man or one party or one nation. It must be a peace which rests on the cooperative effort of the whole world.'

— FRANKLIN D. ROOSEVELT

Arlo Guthrie, following in the footsteps of his protest-singer father, Woody, performs during a music festival at Tufts University in Medford, Massachusetts, in 1969, while a sky-writing pilot makes a peace symbol in the sky.

symbol at an outdoor festival in Massachusetts in 1969 to great effect. Country Joe & The Fish, a folk-rock jug band, released 'Feel-Like-I'm-Fixin'-To-Die Rag' in 1967, and with its, 'What am I fightin' for?' message, it soon became an anthem of the antiwar movement in the USA. Wherever Country Joe performed, there were people with Holtom's symbol painted somewhere on their person.

HIPPIE CHIC
Holtom's symbol became more and more visible among hippies as the 1960s drew to a close. Since their agenda was predominantly anti-Vietnam war, its original message of nuclear disarmament was almost completely lost and

replaced by a representation of antiwar. In the 1970s, the symbol found its way into political campaigns as the anti-Vietnam call began to win votes and badges were produced in the hundreds of thousands, bearing the symbol and an out-of-Asia message. Rock stars such as Neil Young – his custom-made guitar strap featuring the symbol and a dove of peace – and Bob Dylan, who painted the peace icon into the cover image of his 1974 album, *Planet Waves*, continued to give the symbol prominence, but it was also becoming increasingly used by non-hippies, if only to reflect an element of the revolutionary spirit of the 1960s.

Fashion designers wove it and printed it on their shirts, dresses, trousers, and jackets;

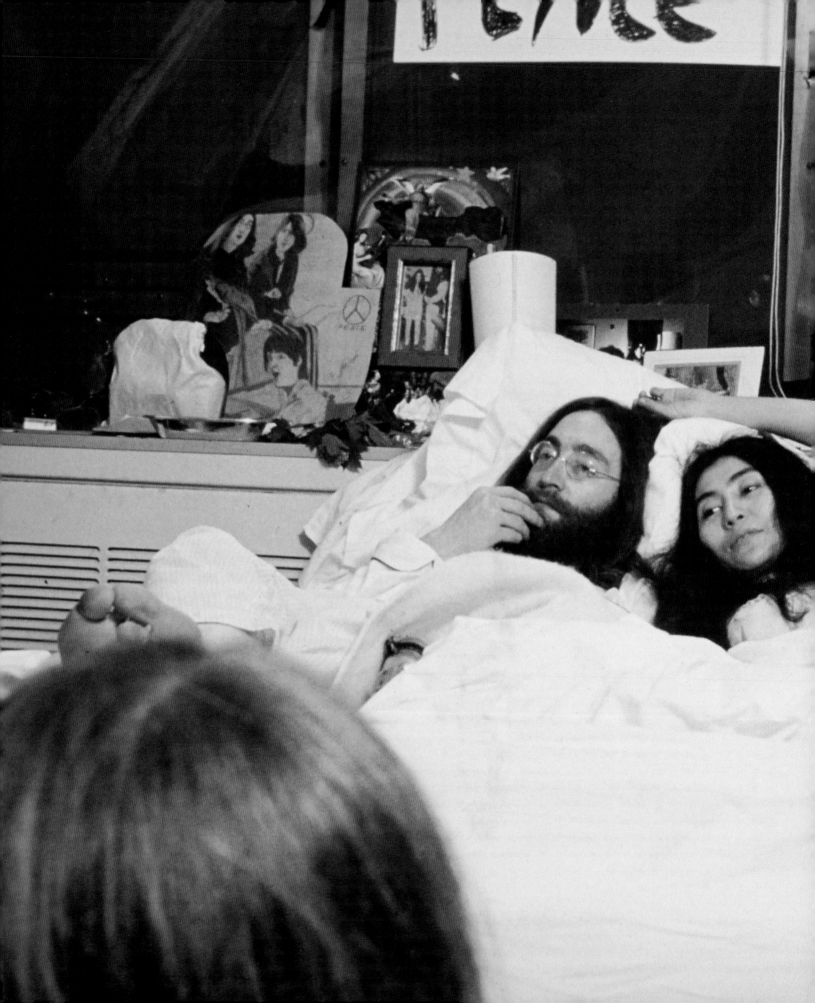

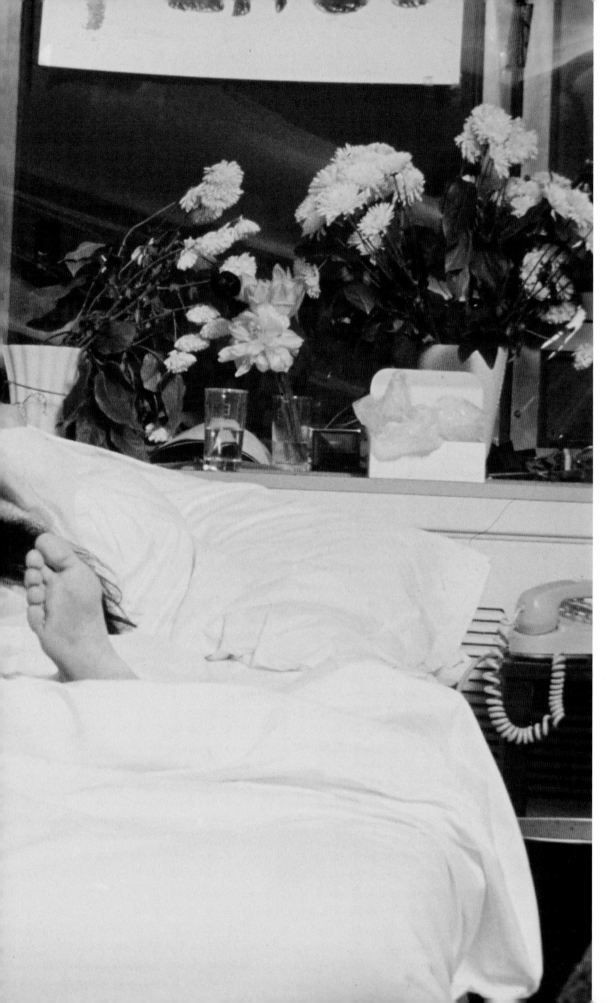

In the spring of 1969, Beatle, John Lennon and his new wife, Yoko Ono, staged a 'bed-in' for peace at Montreal's Queen Elizabeth Hotel – part of their anti-Vietnam war, peace campaign. On 1 June – together with friends, journalists and celebrity peace protesterssuch as Dick Gregory, Tommy Smothers and Timothy Leary – they recorded what would become the unofficial theme song of the peace movement, the Lennon-penned, 'Give Peace a Chance'.

LET THE PEOPLE VOTE ON WAR

VIETNAM REFERENDUM 70

VOTE YES OUT NOW

VIETNAM REFERENDUM 70

CAT LOVERS AGAINST THE BOMB

MARCH AGAINST THE WAR

WOMEN'S CONTINGENT APRIL 24

WASHINGTON DC   SAN FRANCISCO

MAKE LOVE NOT WAR

▲ Peace badges began to appear in numerous variations by the end of the 1960s, from the specific anti-Vietnam war badge to the ubiquitous 'Make Love Not War' badge. Even cat lovers had their say.

▶ Fashion model, Erikk Najarek, models a multicoloured jacket resplendent with peace signs created by New York furrier, George Kaplan, in 1970.

Hippie Necklace

◀ The hippie stereotype has been forever linked to the peace sign. The 'Hippie Necklace' was designed in Italy (and made in China) in 2004.

▶ A Grateful Dead fan is covered in badges – including, of course, the peace sign – at a concert by the band at the Greek Theatre, Berkeley, California, in 1987.

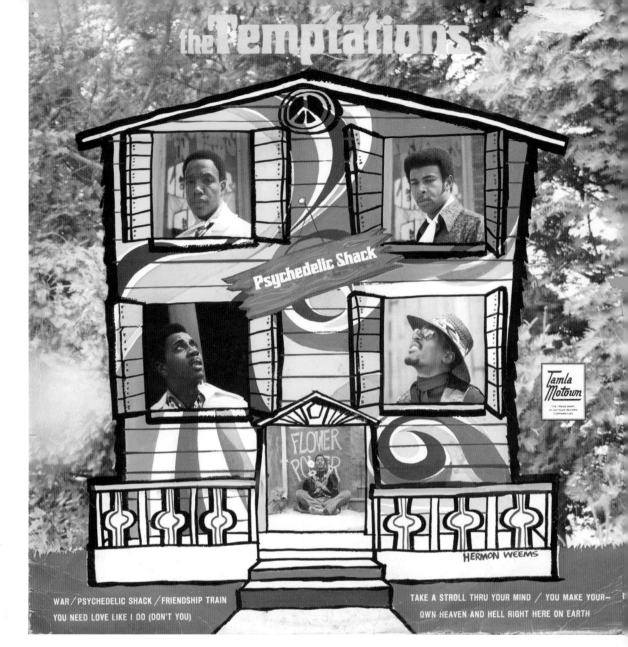

the Temptations

Psychedelic Shack

Flower Power

Tamla Motown
THE TRADE MARK
OF MOTOWN RECORD
CORPORATION

HERMON WEEMS

WAR / PSYCHEDELIC SHACK / FRIENDSHIP TRAIN   TAKE A STROLL THRU YOUR MIND / YOU MAKE YOUR—
YOU NEED LOVE LIKE I DO (DON'T YOU)   OWN HEAVEN AND HELL RIGHT HERE ON EARTH

▶ **Motown vocal group, The Temptations, plugged into flower power in their 1970 album,** *Psychedelic Shack*. **Their use of the peace symbol on the album's cover was a forerunner of its later use by hip-hop artists such as De La Soul.**

◀ **Pianist/composer Mary Lou Williams' 1970 album,** *Music for Peace*, **features an iconic peace-sign sleeve design by the great jazz illustrator, David Stone Martin.**

jewellers made rings, earrings, necklaces and brooches with it to sell at street markets and in small boutiques and bazaars in the West.

At first the symbol was strictly the preserve of alternative fashion designers, but in the 1970s, as hippie chic entered high-end shops, mainstream clothing labels began to display it. The beauty of it for mass-market manufacturers was that not only did it suggest rebellion, which had become of prime importance in cutting-edge street fashion, but also that it was copyright-free and they didn't have to pay for its use.

But by the end of the 1970s, hippies began

to be denigrated by the new wave of punk style across the UK and the USA. As the fashion world latched on to the new images of street revolt – zips, rips and the anarchist symbol of an A in a circle – Holtom's symbol became a no-no. It was too closely associated with an idealism that, as far as the disaffected youth of the late-1970s were concerned, had failed to change the world in any way that related to them. So from being a badge of unity against the world, it became a symbol of self-indulgence and old, outmoded issues. Punks wanted shock value and Holtom's ND was not shocking anymore. It fell from

ORIGINAL MOTION PICTURE SOUNDTRACK

PLATOON

AND SONGS FROM THE ERA

"The Village"
ADAGIO FOR STRINGS
THE VANCOUVER SYMPHONY ORCHESTRA
Conducted by GEORGES DELERUE

TRACKS OF MY TEARS
SMOKEY ROBINSON

OKIE FROM MUSKOGEE
MERLE HAGGARD

HELLO, I LOVE YOU
THE DOORS

WHITE RABBIT
JEFFERSON AIRPLANE

"BARNES SHOOTS ELIAS"
THE VANCOUVER SYMPHONY ORCHESTRA
Conducted by GEORGES DELERUE

RESPECT
ARETHA FRANKLIN

(SITTIN' ON) THE DOCK OF THE BAY
OTIS REDDING

WHEN A MAN LOVES A WOMAN
PERCY SLEDGE

GROOVIN'
THE RASCALS

ADAGIO FOR STRINGS
THE VANCOUVER SYMPHONY ORCHESTRA
Conducted by GEORGES DELERUE

A FILM FROM HEMDALE

widespread use, becoming almost the sole property of American Deadheads – the Grateful Dead fans who followed the band on its seemingly endless treks across the USA in the late-1970s and 1980s and who wore the symbol as their personal logo.

ANARCHY IN THE UK

In stark contrast, in the UK the peace symbol came into wider use among the post-punk anarchist movement, who joined with any and all direct-action protest groups to confront the Thatcher government. From the women's peace

An album of the songs from Oliver Stone's 1987 film, *Platoon*, shows the peace sign worked into the design as part of a soldier's dog tag.

The single sleeve for 'Me Myself and I', the best-known track from the *3 Feet High and Rising* album by De La Soul, features the peace sign as part of the group's name.

HIP HOP FOR PEACE

In the late 1980s the symbol came back into fashion in the USA in a most unexpected place. The South Los Angeles neighbourhood of Compton had become synonymous with black-on-black crime, where gangs killed each other because of the colour of their bandannas and the style of their sneakers. It had also, at the same time as New York, spawned a new type of music – hip hop and rap. Much early rap was 'gangsta' rap, which bragged about shooting people and stealing indiscriminantly. The violent materialism of an enormous underclass, where anyone who survived jail terms became a hero

to younger kids, had swept across the USA and the West, also attracting middle-class white kids who wanted to be 'bad'. But for many African Americans living in underfunded and violent inner cities, the music had become their folk music; its message, 'Kill or be killed'.

ANTIGANGSTA RAP

But there was an alternative to the gun-crazy gangsta sound, and Gerald Holtom's symbol was first used most successfully by De La Soul, a New York trio who mixed flower power symbolism with modern beats in their anti-gangsta rap. Their debut album, *3 Feet High and Rising* (1989),

▶ UK dance outfit Sonz of a Loop Da Loop Era & the Scratchadelic Experience released *Peace & Loveism* in 1992, its sleeve replete with peace-sign imagery.

sonz of a loop da loop era
& the scratchadelic experience

PEACE & LOVEISM

The word 'peace'
in stylised graffiti
is painted next to a
peace symbol on a wall
photographed in Los
Angeles in 1992.

Bruce Springsteen
rehearses in Los Angeles
in 1992 with bass player
Tommy Simms, whose
guitar and strap both
prominently display
the peace sign.

▶ **Always a campaigner for peace, Canadian rock musician, Neil Young, performs with his band Crazy Horse at the 35th Montreux Jazz Festival in Switzerland in 2001.**

◀ **Actress Alyssa Milano wears a potentially provocative peace sign at a 2005 'Rockin' the Corps' concert held as a thank you to American Marines who served in the war in Iraq and Afghanistan.**

displayed Holtom's design, which also became the 'o' in their name on all of their covers, for singles as well as the album. Their success firmly put the symbol in the hip-hop graffiti lexicon, and it began appearing on other record and CD sleeves, as well as on walls in African-American communities where gang warfare was common. It became a symbol of unity and accompanied an antiviolence message for rappers and hip-hop artists who opposed the macho message of

gangsta rappers and called for peace in the neighbourhood. In the 1990s, hip-hop fashion took over, and clothes shops everywhere sold baseball caps, basketball shirts, and bandannas. So Holtom's design again appeared on shirts, jackets and jewellery – now with 'bling' diamonds added. Fashion labels took notice of what hip-hop kids were wearing and also began to put the symbol on their wares. It was hip, had a positive vibe, and no one mentioned hippies anymore.

REMEMBERING THE 1960S

As Holtom's symbol appeared on more CD sleeves and as 1960s anniversaries started to crop up, it became more visible everywhere. It was on T-shirts sold at the 25th anniversary Woodstock concert in 1994 (even more were seen at the 30th anniversary in 1999), was on hundreds of websites, stamped on badges and T-shirts, and came to represent a side of the 1960s worth remembering. This is most obvious on music CDs from the years 1966–1970, which used the symbol as a visual shorthand for 'hippies, flower power, and love'. Then came the war.

WAR IN IRAQ

In 2003, as the USA and UK prepared to remove Saddam Hussein from power in Iraq, there was a huge body of antiwar activism in both countries – which was echoed around the world. Liberal-minded Hollywood stars began wearing Holtom's design to publicly mark their opposition to this –

and any other – war. Tie pins, T-shirts, pendants, jewellery and jackets with the symbol were worn in protest of the war in Iraq. The Gap chain printed it on Christmas shopping bags in the run-up to the war (and again at Christmas 2006) with the slogan 'Love and Peace'. Another million or more badges have been produced bearing the symbol and an antiwar message.

FIFTY YEARS IN FASHION

Fifty years after it was first spotted on buadges and banners, the peace sign is still worn as an antiwar symbol – and in opposition to nuclear weapons, too. It has survived because of its simplicity, its ease of reproduction, and as a positive image despite being a sign of opposition. It's worn by movie actors, hip-hop stars, hippies, punks, fashionistas, the unhip and the unaware, as well as nuclear disarmament and antiwar activists. Unlike anything in the transient world of fashion, it continues to endure.

▲ **A peace sign on his tie allows actor Tim Robbins to make a statement for peace as he arrives at the 77th annual Academy Awards at the Kodak Theatre, Hollywood.**

▶ **Peace was certainly a fashion item at a 2007 Milan runway show that featured this top by Italian design company, Moschino.**

APOCALYPSE NOW?

After the Paris Peace accords of 1973 and the final scramble into the last helicopter fleeing the American embassy in Saigon in 1975, the Vietnam war was at last over. But the opening years of the next decade saw an even more ominous threat to world peace when Ronald Reagan became president in 1981. His plan was to install a force of cruise missiles across Europe as part of his 'Star Wars' strategy, effectively making the USA's allies the front line in a possible nuclear conflagration. The prospect of an atomic apocalypse once more reared its head, and the peace movement was again at the forefront of nonviolent resistance to the war machine. Campaigns sprung up all over Europe, the USA and elsewhere – most memorably in the Women's Peace Camp outside the Greenham Common American missile base in England.

The Reagan era

During the Vietnam war, Hanoi concealed accurate casualty figures to avoid demoralising the public, but figures declassified by the Vietnamese government in 1995 showed that 5.1 million people died in the war with the USA. This included 4 million civilians in North and South Vietnam. Military casualties are put at 1.1 million, with 600,000 wounded. In 2006, the government estimated that there are more than 4 million Vietnamese victims of dioxin poisoning, the result of the USA spraying over 13 percent of the country with Agent Orange. In some areas dioxin levels are over a hundred times the accepted international standard.

Thousands of Laotian civilians and troops were killed in the final conflict and tens of thousands of Cambodians died when the USA bombed their country (attempting to kill fleeing Vietnamese soldiers). Between 500,000 and 2 million people died in the Khmer Rouge-inflicted genocide after the civil war that followed the American destabilization of the Cambodian government. The Vietnam war ended on 30 April 1975, with an undignified scramble for places on the last helicopter to leave the roof of the American embassy in Saigon, though few actual American troops had been in the country since the Paris Peace accords were signed in 1973. There have been many studies done since the war, suggesting that antiwar groups played a significant role in the ending of the conflict by influencing public opinion.

THE 'EVIL EMPIRE'

Antiwar activity inevitably slowed down in the USA after the final withdrawal, only to revive again in the 1980s when the American government began saber-rattling once more. On 20 January 1981, Ronald Reagan became President of the USA. As a lifelong anti-Communist of the old school, Reagan scrapped the policy of *détente* – 'peaceful coexistence' – with the Soviets and adopted in its place a much harder line in dealing with the 'evil empire'. He first used the term to describe the USSR on 8 March 1983, in a speech to the National Association of Evangelicals.

Reagan's predecessor, Jimmy Carter, had been deeply worried by the existence of 243 Soviet triple-headed SS-20 Saber missiles targeted at western Europe. He planned to counter them by deploying ground-launched cruise missiles (GLCMs) and Pershing II missiles across Europe, aimed at the USSR.

Ground-launched cruise missiles combined with the Pershing IIs were a potent combination. The GLCM missiles were slow but hard to detect because they were mobile and could be launched from the back of trucks that could travel in convoy well away from any Soviet-targeted air force base. Two hours after they were on their way, they could be followed by a Pershing strike. The Pershings were so fast that no response was possible before their targets were annihilated.

Reagan told the UK parliament in 1982 that he intended to ' ... consign the Soviet Union to the ash heap of history'. He claimed that escalating the arms race would be so expensive that the Russians would be forced to negotiate for a reduction in the number of warheads. It seemed to many Europeans and to Americans familiar with his extreme anti-Communist cold war rhetoric, that Reagan was preparing for a tactical nuclear war to be fought on European territory.

Tomahawk cruise missiles reach the end of the production line at the General Dynamics Convair factory in San Diego in 1989 before being shipped to the American Navy.

In 1982, the San Francisco-based Educomics published an English-language version of a Japanese comic book, written and drawn by a genuine Hiroshima survivor, Keiji Nakazawa. Called, *I Saw It: The Atomic Bombing of Hiroshima*, its aim was to bring home to a future generation, via comic-book form, the true horror of nuclear weapons.

A Tomahawk cruise missile in flight. The weapon has seen more than a quarter century of service since first being deployed in Europe in the early 1980s.

All across Europe mass protests erupted when the governments of the Netherlands, Italy, Germany, Belgium and Britain agreed to allow the USA to base Tomahawk GLCMs and Pershing IIs in their countries, ensuring that those countries would be targets for Soviet SS-20s.

On 14 November 1983, the UK government voted to allow the 303rd Tactical Missile Wing to be based at RAF Molesworth, near Cambridge, and the 501st Tactical Missile Wing to be installed at RAF Greenham Common. On 16 November in Italy, the 487th Tactical Missile Wing was permitted to be based at Comiso. On 22 November, the West German parliament approved the use of the Wuenschen Air Base by the 38th Tactical Missile Wing; the Belgians got the 485th Tactical Missile Wing at the air base at Florennes. The 486th Tactical Missile Wing was based at Woensdrecht in the Netherlands. The training facility for them all was at Davis-Monthan Air Force Base in Arizona. The day after the West Germans gave their approval, the Soviets walked out of the talks on reducing intermediate range nuclear forces.

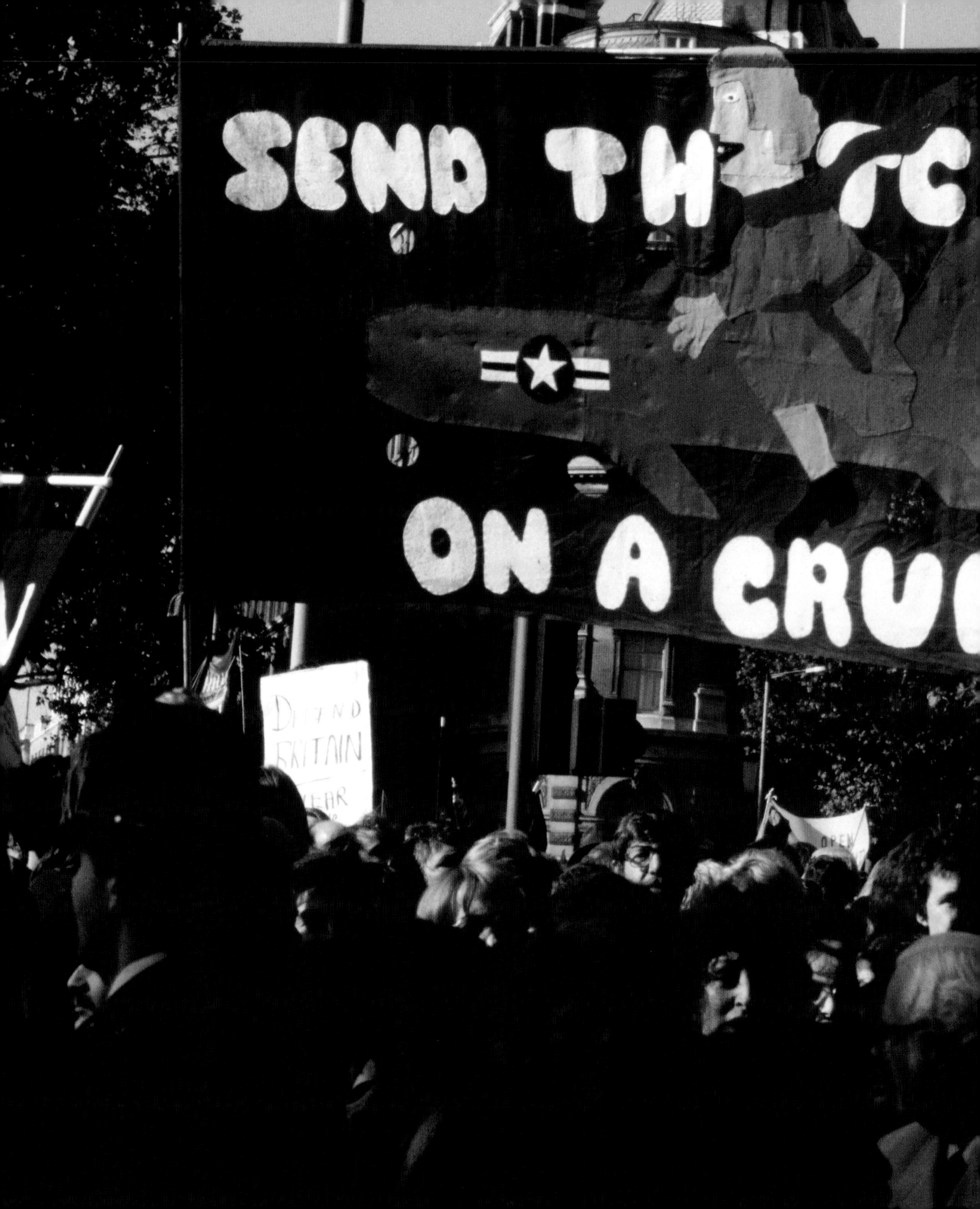
SEND TH TC
ON A CRU
DEFEND
BRITAIN

Anticruise missile protesters march in London in 1983, their banner declaring 'Send Thatcher on a Cruise'.

STAR WARS

On 23 March 1983, Reagan announced that he had instructed scientists to research and build a missile shield for the USA, the Strategic Defence Initiative, a project that quickly became known as Star Wars, but which, if it worked, would mean that the USA could launch a first-strike attack without being destroyed in return; Reagan was undermining the 'mutual assured destruction' (MAD) balance of power that had so far prevented a nuclear exchange. Many people in both the USA and USSR were concerned that the Strategic Defence Initiative went against the Antiballistic Missile Treaty signed by Richard Nixon and Leonid Brezhnev in 1972.

The Soviets were horrified at Reagan's military buildup and casual references to nuclear war and responded by breaking off arms-control talks and resuming the placement of SS-20 series nuclear missiles, which had been shelved during the talks. New missile silos were therefore built in Czechoslovakia and East Germany. Soviet nuclear submarines nestling deep in the ocean and beneath Arctic ice were moved closer to the USA's coastlines. The Kremlin's five-year plan published in 1984 incorporated a 45 percent increase in military spending. 'The impact of Reagan's hard line policy … was exactly the opposite of the one intended by Washington', recalled Anatoly Dobrynin, the long-time Soviet ambassador to the USA. 'It strengthened those in the Politburo, the Central Committee and the security apparatus who had been pressing for a mirror image of Reagan's own policy.'

PEACE CAMP

There was an immediate response to the news that the USA intended to install cruise and Pershing missiles in Europe. In September 1981, a group of women marched from Cardiff, Wales, to the Greenham Common air base near Newbury in Berkshire, west of London, where they set up a peace camp. They lived in 'benders', a traditional temporary shelter used by shepherds,

Protests against cruise and Pershing missiles in Britain were many and varied; here CND supporters march through London in October 1983.

> '**Establishing lasting peace is the work of education; all politics can do is keep us out of war.**'
>
> — MARIA MONTESSORI

made by bending living trees over and using them as the support for a plastic tarpaulin that was then staked to the ground or held by large rocks like a tent. The women made them comfortable, lining them with blankets and layers of plastic to act as insulation, and decorating them with wildflowers and photographs of boyfriends, husbands and children. Local farmers brought bales of straw, which they covered with blankets to use as mattresses. They all had sleeping bags. The benders were lit by candles, usually three or four on a saucer. Supporters turned up every day with blankets, food, and drink (alcoholic and otherwise), which was very welcome.

SABOTAGE

Although parliament had not yet given permission for the missiles to be based in Britain, the USA knew that the UK government would acquiesce and had already begun building hardened silos for the missiles at the base. The women did their best to sabotage construction work by blockading the gates and cutting holes in the perimeter fence to stage sit-ins on the construction site. The Greenham Common Women's Peace Camp became a focal point for antinuclear activity in Britain throughout the 1980s. Large numbers of women would be summoned for specific events. One of the biggest, and for many people the greatest demonstration at Greenham Common, was in December 1982 when more than 30,000 women gathered at the base and joined hands around its perimeter fence. The action was called 'Embrace the Base'.

EMBRACE THE BASE

In the summer of 1982, one of the Greenham Common women, Barbara Doris, visited the USA and participated in a protest at the Pentagon where women held hands and encircled the building. There had been a famous demonstration like this in the 1960s, when hippies thought that by encircling the Pentagon, they could make it levitate. It didn't move even a centimetre off the ground. It did, however, move Barbara Doris, and she returned to Britain to tell the women at the

Women at the Greenham Common site sing as they link arms around the cruise missile base.

Blocking the gates of the missile base, the Greenham Common protesters tie themselves together with wool, much to the annoyance of the police and military trying to move them.

A group of the Greenham Common Peace Camp women gather in an improvised 'sitting room' on the leafy outskirts of the proposed cruise missile base.

camp about the protest. Greenham Common was 14.5 km (9 miles) in circumference and seemed too large to encircle, but with enough women it was possible. It was camper Lyn Jones who ended the meeting by saying, 'Let's do it!'.

It was a last-minute decision in late October that didn't give the organisers much time. The demonstration was scheduled for 12 December, the anniversary of the decision to allow cruise missiles into Britain, and was organised by chain letter. Each of the original organisers sent out ten letters, and the recipients were expected to do the same to their friends and contacts.

On the appointed day 30,000 women turned up. All over the west of England, roads were jammed with buses bringing women to Greenham Common, all waving suffragette coloured ribbons.

The action may have been naïve, but it built a great spirit of solidarity among the participants. In a palpable sense the women were countering the negativity of nuclear weapons with a positive spirit of creativity and life affirmation. The peace camp could always be reduced to a simple equation of life versus death. They all brought gifts – things that symbolised life and countered the negative impact of the base. Soon the entire fence was covered with flowers, paintings, babies' nappies, photographs of children, pictures of their houses or gardens, cutouts of doves, knitted items and embroidery. One woman hung her wedding dress on the fence. Someone attached a whole, beautiful dinner service to the fence. And, of course, there were many different variations of the peace symbol.

The Greenham women lived for the duration of their peace campaign in hundreds of 'benders' – tents made by bending living trees and covering them with tarpaulin.

EMBROIDERY FOR PEACE

Women began to embroider the fence and this became a major Greenham theme. 'The soldiers would become absurdly enraged by embroidery when women darned the fence', recalled participant Ann Pettitt. 'They'd darn huge areas of it in the following years; darning would become something they would do with multi-coloured wool and everything. They darned such enormous areas of it that you couldn't see through it. The military would be sent with scissors to cut through these silly bits of darning, and then they'd reappear the next morning.'

THE ZENITH

The Imperial War Museum has tapes of some of the women describing the event. Ann Pettitt says: 'Embrace the Base; I always think of that as the kind of zenith, the high spot of the whole Greenham story really, because that was when the original message went thumping round the world. The good that it did was done that day and everything that had gone before seemed to have been entirely necessary to the creation of that day. That was when the message did get through the media and it got through on the mass media in a completely simple, direct way … That was the best day of my life, that was brilliant, that was amazing … I just cried.'

As the USA knew they would, the British government signed the cruise missile agreement, and within days the missiles began to arrive from the States. The women continued to protest, facing long days in court, fines, even prison for their actions. The Newbury District Council tried to close the camp by evicting them, but always in vain. Inevitably the camp's population dwindled, but a hard core remained. It was 19 years before

Demonstrators tug at the Greenham Common perimeter fence in a coordinated attempt (not entirely unsuccessful) to pull it down.

A female demonstrator
is arrested as a friend
pleads for her release
during protests at
Greenham Common,
in December 1983.

the last of the Greenham Common protesters left the base, in September 2000. They stuck rigidly to the ideals of nonviolent direct action throughout their time at the site. When one protester picked up a stone, four others rushed over and explained that she must not throw it. As long as they were nonviolent, they could never be successfully evicted. They learned to ignore all the taunts and sexist comments thrown at them, no matter how provocative.

A WOMEN'S PROTEST

Because it was a uniquely women's protest, imaginative methods of nonviolence evolved. The women webbed each other together, for instance, completely confusing the police. The new missiles required a large staff, so extra sewage lines had to be laid to the camp, giving the women many ways to disrupt operations. They lay across the ditch, tied to each other with wool, making it more difficult to drag them away.

As Ann Pettitt explained in her interview for the Imperial War Museum: 'All they needed was a pair of scissors for God's sake, but they just didn't know how or where to begin approaching this new thing you see and it took them ages to move them away, and they lost a whole day's work and everything because the women were tied up with wool. It was as simple as that. There were so many different ways, I suppose, that you could sort of outwit and startle the authorities, rather than this kind of brutish, unintelligent head-on clash between completely unequal forces, in which you would inevitably be the loser. It never seemed to me to make a lot of sense. I mean nonviolent protest, as a form of protest, is much more intelligent, isn't it?'

'BLACK CARDIGANS'

For months the women snipped away at the wire fence in places where they wouldn't be noticed. Then, on Halloween, they announced a party with picnics and fires, witches broomsticks and pointed hats. At the appointed time the code word 'Black Cardigans', (meaning bolt cutters) which only the women understood, was given. At 4:00 P.M. the word went around and in the middle of the party, the women ran to the fence and cut down the remaining wire. So much had already been weakened that all they had to do was climb on each other's shoulders to clip the top of the wire and down it came.

'In peace sons bury fathers, but war violates the order of nature, and fathers bury sons.'

— HERODOTUS

POST-APOCALYPSE MOVIES

Simultaneous with the evolution of the peace movement and universal recognition of the peace symbol, after-Armageddon stories have emerged in books and films. Typical of these are the 1965 BBC TV-drama, *The War Game*, the American television film, *The Day After* (1983), and – projecting the scenario far into the future – the first of the *Planet of the Apes* films (1968). One of the most successful was made in 1980 by director George Miller; *Mad Max*, was an Australian post-atomic war film starring the then-unknown Mel Gibson. Its apocalyptic story of social breakdown, murder, and vengeance was hugely popular and led to two sequels – *Mad Max 2: The Road Warrior* in 1982 and *Mad Max Beyond Thunderdrome* in 1985.

MAD MAX

Produced by
BYRON KENNEDY

Directed by
GEORGE MILLER

With
MEL GIBSON

Music by
BRIAN MAY

Written by
JAMES McCAUSLAND and **GEORGE MILL**

British Labour Party leader, Neil Kinnock, in front of Peter Kennard's adapted logo of a Trident missile bursting through the peace sign, at the anti-cruise missile protest in London's Hyde Park, in October 1983.

'We shall never be able to effect physical disarmament until we have succeeded in effecting moral disarmament.'

— J. RAMSAY MACDONALD

Almost half the fence fell. The police inside were furious. With no jurisdiction on the outside, they had to stand and watch as it came tumbling down. The few police outside were outnumbered 60 or 70 to 1. Thalia Campbell recalled the event: 'It took them about 20 minutes to work out their strategy for coping with this. They would arrest one woman, and then there were 59 still cutting the fence down, so they would let her go and grab hold of another one, let that one go and the fence was still being chopped down. Finally, after about 20 minutes, they decided to take the bolt cutters off us and throw them into the base. By that time so much damage had been done, they got the helicopters out and were actually flying the helicopters at us, trying to blow us off the fence.'

There were many more protests and prison sentences. In April 1983, 70,000 people staged a demonstration linking Burghfield, Aldermaston and Greenham Common in a human chain that stretched 22km (14 miles), while 200 women, dressed as furry animals, entered the missile base and held a protest picnic. In December 1983,

A protester is arrested by police during a 1983 demonstration against the deployment of Pershing missiles in Ramstein, Germany.

Greenham was circled once more and this time 50,000 women demonstrated, holding up mirrors so that members of the war machine could see themselves. Again, sections of fence toppled.

EUROPE AGAINST CRUISE
There were plenty of demonstrations in other European countries against cruise and Trident missiles. In the Netherlands a legal petition by 20,000 plaintiffs took the government to court to prevent the stationing of missiles on Dutch soil, but with only limited success. The petition delayed, but didn't stop, the missiles' deployment.

On 12 January 1987, a blockade of a USAF base at Mutlangen in West Germany to protest against the deployment of Pershing missiles was staged by 22 judges. When in court, they told fellow judges they had a special responsibility not to be silent in the face of growing stockpiles of nuclear weapons. 'It is our office to serve justice and peace', explained judge Ulf Panzer. 'Nuclear arms do not serve justice or peace. They are the ultimate crime. They hold all humankind

'All we are saying is give peace a chance.'

– JOHN LENNON

Protesters carry the peace sign in 1985 at the Waterton-Glacier International Peace Park on the American-Canadian border.

CND led the campaign against the National Missile Defence System – nicknamed Son of Star Wars – in this 2001 demonstration outside the Ministry of Defence in London.

as hostages.' The International group of Physicians for the Prevention of Nuclear War (IPPNW) were awarded the Nobel Peace Prize in 1985. By that time their organisation had the support of 140,000 doctors in 34 countries and had successfully lobbied the World Health Assembly to refer the issue to the World Court.

THE WORLD AGAINST CRUISE

In the USA, 150,000 marched in Washington to protest against the deployment of GLCMs. The protests involved figures such as pediatrician, Benjamin Spock, who, at a demonstration at Cape Canaveral Air Force Station in Florida on 17 January 1987, climbed over the barbed-wire fence to protest against the test firing of a Trident II missile.

Apparently, Reagan was concerned about the opposition to missiles on European soil and early in his presidency began to change his stance. He wrote to Soviet leader, Leonid Brezhnev, suggesting they begin a dialogue, but Brezhnev died soon after. Then Brezhnev's successor, Yuri Andropov, died in February 1984 before any talks could take place. And the next Communist Party general secretary, Konstantin Chernenko, died in 1985.

WITHDRAWAL

Talks finally began in 1985 and two years later Reagan and the Soviet president, Mikhail Gorbachev, signed the Intermediate-range Nuclear Forces (INF) Treaty, which eliminated an entire class of nuclear weapons. This would mean the final removal of cruise missiles from Greenham Common and the other contentious European bases.

The Greenham Common Peace Camp, however, had become a focal point in Britain for the entire antinuclear issue and remained as a continuing protest against nuclear weapons until September 2000, when the last of the women left the base. Now part of Greenham Common has been converted into a business park, with the rest returning to common land, open to all.

PEACE NOW!

The evolution of Gerald Holtom's symbol from just a ban-the-bomb sign
to a universal icon for peace began in the 1960s, with its widespread use in
protests against the war in Vietnam. The logo gained its widest exposure via
demonstrations such as the huge American moratorium protests in 1969 and
similar events around the world. It was later seen on graffiti-covered walls in
a Los Angeles ghetto, in Argentinian protests against the Falklands war, on the
collapsing Berlin Wall and on the faces of aboriginal Australians resisting
uranium mining on their lands. As a cipher for radical youth, it continued to
appear wherever the young gathered, from the revived Woodstock festival to
the annual UK rock gathering at Glastonbury. And it acquired a new potency
in the early 21st century with the Anglo-American invasion of Iraq.

Universal icon

By the end of the 1980s, the peace symbol was no longer just an icon for the struggle against nuclear weapons; it had become a worldwide shorthand for peace itself. This long process involved a protest outside the British government's Porton Down Biological Warfare station, in 1965. Banners bearing the peace sign had slogans that read 'No Germ Warfare', taking the focus away from the sign's semaphore message of nuclear disarmament into a more general area of meaning. The symbol had been used by the Greek Committee of 100 in 1963, but their protest – like early British protests – was against American nuclear bases on Greek soil.

By the late 1960s the sign was appropriated in the USA to protest against the war in Vietnam. Prominent at a large anti-Vietnam war rally held in New York in April 1967, its use had spread so sufficiently that the public understood what was being said in October 1967 when Bishop James A. Pike, former bishop of the Episcopal Diocese of San Francisco, held up a peace symbol medallion and told a meeting: 'I have pledged to wear this until we cease our invasion of Vietnam.' By then it was in wide circulation across the country, and whenever government representatives spoke in public, the peace symbol was usually there, hand-drawn on a placard, calling for the end to American involvement in the Vietnam war.

The most extensive use came with the moratorium marches in the autumn of 1969. On 29 April 1969, David Hawk, a divinity student on leave from Union Theological Seminary, who was active in Eugene McCarthy's presidential campaign and who had recently refused military induction, had a meeting in the White House Situation Room with top Nixon administration officials, Henry Kissinger and John Ehrlichman. Hawk led a group of campus newspaper editors and antiwar student-body presidents.

As they left the White House, the student leaders told the press: 'We have to resume our efforts to stop the war, because these people aren't going to.' At the same time, a Boston businessman, Jerome Grossman, suggested a series of short monthly general strikes timed to begin if the war was not ended by the October. He said it would 'enable a broad segment of the American people to participate in a legal and traditional protest action which will have a painful effect upon all with power and influence'. This was not as fantastic as it sounded because, by this time, Americans were two-to-one in favour of bringing their troops home.

MORATORIUM

The idea of a strike was too confrontational for many antiwar activists and organisers David Hawk and Sam Brown reverted to a more acceptable concept: to hold a moratorium on college campuses throughout the country on 15 October, using the meetings to recruit for a larger protest to be held a month later. They hoped to have escalating monthly meetings, but in the form of discussion groups, talks and awareness meetings rather than street protests. They formed the Vietnam Moratorium Committee and opened shop in Washington. Hawk said: 'Our strategy got blown out of the water, because it caught on like wildfire.'

The idea struck just the right balance for Americans who didn't want to be associated with anything illegal or radical. As veteran peace activist Sidney Peck explained, the moratorium

The earliest instance of the peace sign being used outside the context of nuclear disarmament was this demonstration in 1965 at the British government's biological warfare plant at Porton Down.

NO
GERM
WARFARE

COMMITTEE OF 100 SALISBURY JUNE 29
TO VISIT PORTON GERM WARFARE STATION

THIS
VIVISEC

AGAINST
THE GERMS
OF WAR

NO
GERM
WARFARE

PORTON
GERM WARFARE

WICKED

WASTE OF
BRAIN & MONEY

'It isn't enough to talk about peace, one must believe in it. And it isn't enough to believe in it, one must work at it.'

– ELEANOR ROOSEVELT

Demonstrators wave
a peace flag near the
Washington Monument
in Washington, DC,
during the observance
of the moratorium
in 1969.

'allowed people to express their opposition to the war in a way that was comfortable. It could be wearing an armband, it could be honking your horn, it could be leaving your lights on. No matter what your politics were, if you were against the war, here was a chance to express it.' The moratorium was about discussion, a chance to debate the issues and a chance for ordinary people to make their feelings public.

A GREAT START
The first day of demonstrations, on 15 October 1969, was a clear success. Future president, Bill Clinton, then studying at Oxford University on a Rhodes Scholarship, organised a protest in England – which would cause some problems for him later when he ran for the White House.

The largest demonstration was in Boston, where 100,000 listened to an anti-Vietnam war speech by Senator George McGovern. All across the country, schoolchildren and students, office and factory workers, activists and faith groups took part in candlelit vigils, rallies, readings of the names of dead American troops, religious services and 'teach-ins', school seminars and public meetings. All wore black armbands to show dissent and pay tribute to Americans killed in the war since 1961.

Moratorium committees were formed by employees working at all the major newspapers, TV stations and publishing houses. Lab workers and secretaries at the Massachusetts Institute of Technology in Boston formed committees, as did people in government agencies in Washington. Committee members ran the discussions, teach-ins, and recruitment meetings, although often faced with antagonism from their bosses. *The New York Times*, for instance, refused the committee use of its auditorium for 15 October, as did the National Institute for Mental Health.

ILLINOIS
Activities at the University of Illinois in Champaign were typical. In September the faculty senate approved a 30-minute moratorium of classes on 15 October to allow students and faculty to discuss the war. However, the College of Liberal Arts and Sciences cancelled all classes, and 9,000 people marched to West Side Park to protest. And 5,000 people listened to speeches from singer Eartha Kitt and Illinois State Supreme Court Justice William G. Clark at the University's Illinois Union building. *Life* described it as 'a display without historical parallel, the largest expression of public dissent ever seen in this country'.

WASHINGTON
The 15 October demonstration was followed a month later, on 15 November, by an even bigger initiative to protest against the war. An estimated 2 million Americans took part in what was believed to be the largest demonstration in the USA's history. The focal point of the protests was Washington, DC, with more than 40 different events involving over 500,000 demonstrators.

For some the rally began the night before with a candlelit vigil on the steps of the Capitol, but for many it was with the completion of a solemn 40-hour 'March Against Death', when 40,000 people filed past the White House, each carrying the name of an American soldier killed in Vietnam. They were kept from the White House by a solid wall of buses parked along the side of the road between them and President Nixon's home.

All the landmarks in Washington were guarded by hundreds of heavily armed troops. From a stage near the White House, three American senators – Democrats, Eugene McCarthy and George S. McGovern, and Republican, Charles E. Goodell – addressed the crowds, as did Coretta Scott King (widow of Martin Luther King, Jr), comedian and activist, Dick Gregory, and composer, Leonard Bernstein.

The crowd was entertained by a succession of celebrity artists, including Arlo Guthrie; Pete Seeger; John Denver; Mitch Miller; Peter, Paul, and Mary; and the touring cast of the Broadway musical *Hair*.

'Effete Snobs' (quoting Vice President Spiro Agnew) were just one of the more esoteric (and self-deprecating) subgroups who voiced opposition to the Vietnam war during the moratorium protest.

'Peace is not an absence of war, it is a virtue, a state of mind, a disposition for benevolence, confidence, justice.'

— BARUCH SPINOZA

Addressing the rally in Washington, DC, child-care expert Dr Benjamin Spock said the war was a 'total abomination' that was crippling the USA and must be stopped. In Boston, Senator Edward Kennedy demanded that American combat troops be withdrawn from Vietnam by October 1970 and all forces by the end of 1972.

ADMINISTRATION RESPONSE

The administration attempted to demean supporters of the moratorium. General Wheeler, chairman of the Joint Chiefs of Staff, labelled the demonstrators 'interminably vocal youngsters, strangers alike to soap and reason'. Vice President Spiro Agnew called them: 'Communist dupes comprised of an effete corps of impudent snobs who characterise themselves as intellectuals.' (Agnew was later to resign in disgrace after being indicted for accepting bribes and evading taxes.) In New York, firefighters, police officers and other groups drove with their headlights on to show their support for Nixon and to protest against New York mayor John

Lindsay's decision to fly all city flags at half mast that day.

Despite involving a large number of people, the demonstration in Washington was almost entirely peaceful. There were a few arrests when police decided to remove Black Power activists, but most trouble was elsewhere in the country. In Portland, Oregon, for example, 400 protesters clashed with police as they tried to occupy an army induction centre.

All across Europe, protesters gathered outside American embassies to support the moratorium. The biggest overseas support came later, on 8 May 1970, when over 100,000 people protested in Melbourne, Australia. Some 100,000 people also protested in other Australian cities.

MY LAI

It was the day after the moratorium, 16 November, that the American Army first discussed the My Lai massacre, another occasion for people to express their opprobrium. In March 1970 the army charged 14 officers with suppressing

A 'stars and stripes' flag with the peace sign in place of the stars is held aloft at the moratorium protest, 15 November 1969.

'Peace may sound simple – one beautiful word – but it requires everything we have, every quality, every strength, every dream, every high ideal.'

– YEHUDI MENUHIN (VIOLINIST, CONDUCTOR)

information about the mass killing of civilians on 16 March 1968, when Charlie Company, under the command of Lt. William Calley, entered the Vietnamese village of My Lai and killed more than 300 unarmed women, children and elderly villagers. There had been no resistance. Although he was sentenced to life in prison, Calley was released in 1974.

DUCK HOOK

It seems that the first moratorium led Nixon to cancel Operation Duck Hook, a secret operation planned by Nixon and Kissinger without the knowledge of Secretary of Defence, Melvin Laird.

According to Tom Wells in *The War Within: America's Battle Over Vietnam*, it called for the bombing of Hanoi and other Vietnamese cities and military targets; the bombing of North Vietnam's dike system; its main rail links with China; the mining of harbours and rivers; and the destruction, possibly with low-yield nuclear devices, of the major passes along the Ho-Chi Minh Trail. Duck Hook would last four days and would be repeated, if necessary. Nixon was also considering a plan to drop tactical nuclear weapons on Vietnam's railroad lines.

Nixon had given the Vietnamese a 1 November ultimatum, but the widespread support for the moratorium by the middle classes and the media meant that an operation like Duck Hook would be fiercely opposed, and not just by students.

With opposition raging in the USA, the Vietnamese would feel confident in resisting their latest attack. 'Nixon himself was deeply distressed by the moratorium', wrote Wells. 'His fear that it would undercut his 1 November ultimatum to Hanoi had intensified in the days leading up to the protest, as momentum for it

The liberal democrat politician, George McGovern, who had taken part in the 1969 Washington antiwar rally, was caricatured carrying a peace sign flag during the run-up to the 1972 presidential election. He ran on an anti-Vietnam war ticket against President Richard Nixon.

The incursion into traditional habitats by modern society has never been more pronounced in recent times than in the homelands of native Australian aboriginals, seen here displaying the peace sign as they protest the mining of uranium on their territories in 1985.

had swelled.' Nixon wrote in his memoirs: 'Although publicly I continued to ignore the raging antiwar controversy, I had to face the fact that it ... probably destroyed the credibility of my ultimatum.' Nancy Zaroulis and Gerald Sullivan concluded in *Who Spoke Up?: American Protest Against the War in Vietnam 1963–1975*: 'The anti-war sentiment generated and aired in the fall of 1969 made it politically impossible for the President to proceed with his plan. As a result, thousands, perhaps hundreds of thousands of North Vietnamese and American lives were spared.'

UNIVERSAL CONSCIOUSNESS

By now the peace symbol had entered universal consciousness: It was to be seen daubed on the Berlin Wall, as graffiti in the Los Angeles ghetto and accompanying antigovernment slogans on the walls of towns in Algeria. Sicilian antiwar protesters in Messina had it in 1979, and Argentinian students used it calling for an end to the war with the UK over the Malvinas (Falkland) Islands in 1982. It was in use at a rally in Washington to protest against American involvement in El Salvador in July 1983, and at protests against the American invasion of Grenada in the West Indies that same year; even aboriginal antinuclear activists used it, painting it on their faces as a protest against uranium mining in their territories in Australia in 1985. It was used in a Yugoslavian candlelit vigil in a protest in front of the Romanian embassy in Belgrade. It was worn on T-shirts in Ho Chi Minh City, drawn large in the snows of the Arctic and in the sands of the Sahara. Surfers-for-Peace also drew it in the sand.

Anti-NATO protesters waved a huge peace-symbol flag during demonstrations in Prague in November 2002; a Greenpeace activist at the NATO summit in Istanbul in 2004 had it painted across his T-shirt; and the Greenpeace flagship vessel, *Rainbow Warrior*, had a huge symbol painted on her deck, which was easily visible from the air. In October 2001 in Berlin, thousands

Paintings on display at the 1994 Woodstock revival, held at Saugerties, New York, promote 'peace, love, and flower power', just as earlier artwork had at the now legendary 1969 event.

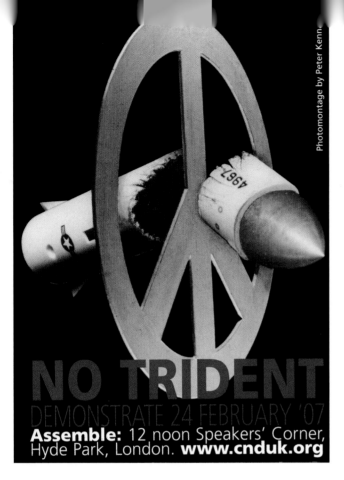

NO TRIDENT
DEMONSTRATE 24 FEBRUARY '07

Assemble: 12 noon Speakers' Corner,
Hyde Park, London. **www.cnduk.org**

Say no to nuclear weapons

DAMON ALBARN · Dirty pretty things · ATHLETE · THOM YORKE
Belle and Sebastian · FRANZ FERDINAND · Noisettes · JARVIS COCKER
KAISER CHIEFS | SUPERGRASS · Babyshambles · The Hours
MASSIVE ATTACK · THE MAGIC NUMBERS · LOSTPROPHETS · SWAYS · BLOC PARTY. · RAZORLIGHT
THE CRIBS · PRIMAL SCREAM · MOGWAI · :BATTLE:
BRITISH SEA POWER · MAXÏMO PARK · ELBOW · JEREMY WARMSLEY
BRAINTAX · Mystery Jets · Richard Hawley · Roots Manuva · the longcut
ASIAN DUB FOUNDATION · Ian Brown · SUPER FURRY ANIMALS · SCRITTI POLITTI · THE ZUTONS · ARCHIE BRONSON OUTFIT
the chemical brothers · Los Campesinos! · APHEX TWIN
DOVES · GET CAPE. WEAR CAPE. FLY · guillemots · The PADDINGTONS
KING BISCUIT TIME · MENSWEAR · Piltomatic
minotaur shock · SNOW PATROL · BOARDS OF CANADA · zero 7

THE government is pressing ahead with a replacement of Trident – Britain's nuclear weapons system. These are Weapons of Mass Destruction which can kill hundreds of millions of people. They cannot protect us from today's security threats such as terrorism and climate change.

Almost 60% of the British public say they don't want Trident replaced. A decision to replace it would make the world a more dangerous place and reinforce the hypocrisy of our government which invaded Iraq on the basis of lies about Weapons of Mass Destruction – but now plans to build its own new nuclear weapons.

If Britain says it needs nuclear weapons for its security, other countries are likely to follow suit. To replace Trident, when we face no nuclear threat, could start a nuclear arms race.

The £76 billion cost to replace and maintain Trident would be better spent on health care, education, alleviating global poverty or tackling the problems of climate change. **Let's choose peace and justice, not nuclear weapons and war.** Join us in calling on the government – No Trident Replacement!

JOIN CND TODAY!
Visit www.cnduk.org for more details

CND

▲ **The war in Iraq and the British government's decision to replace the Trident missile system were met with a huge surge in support for CND in the UK, with Holtom's symbol again being adapted in a visually striking fashion.**

◄ **An estimated 200,000 marchers showed up at a rally in Montreal to protest against the start of the Iraq war in March 2003. Five months later Montreal hosted the annual World Trade Organisation meeting amid thousands of anti-globalisation protesters.**

marched behind the symbol to protest against American air strikes in Afghanistan; it was used in protests over Bosnia in London; and a Filipino painted it on his face in July 2006 during a Manila demonstration urging the government to bring home workers from Lebanon before they were killed in fighting there.

And the symbol has a special place in hippie hearts, with the big rock festivals still a natural home for it. There were far more peace signs at the 1994 Woodstock revival than at the original in 1969, a sign of how far the symbol has come. And at the huge 2007 Glastonbury Festival in southwest England, it was on everything from flags to the outsize single earring worn by Gossip singer Beth Ditto.

WAR IN IRAQ

In the new century the peace symbol has been evident worldwide in opposition to George W. Bush's invasion of Iraq. Many people felt that they were being lied to about the reasons for the war and remained unconvinced that Baghdad

possessed weapons of mass destruction. On 15 February 2003, a coordinated day of antiwar protests was planned all around the world.

According to BBC News, between 6 and 10 million people took part in protests in about 800 cities in up to 60 countries. Some estimates put the figure as high as 30 million, others at 15. Europe was the centre of the biggest protests; the one in Rome, for instance, involved approximately 3 million people and is listed in the 2004 edition of the *Guinness Book of World Records* as the biggest antiwar rally ever held. The demonstration in London that day began with a march organised by the Stop the War Coalition, the CND and the Muslim Association of Britain.

The 5.6-km (3½-mile-long) march, displaying slogans (including the memorable 'Make Tea Not War') with Holtom's ubiquitous peace symbol, was ordered to start early by the police, who were concerned by the crushing numbers already assembled. People arrived by bus and train from 250 cities and towns across Britain.

▲ Over 3,000 people formed a torchlit peace sign in Budapest during an anti-Iraq war rally in 2006.

◄ Protesters called for the impeachment of George W. Bush at a 2003 antiwar protest in Washington, DC.

LONDON

The police estimated that 750,000 people were on the march. Marchers made their way down Piccadilly chanting slogans, banging drums and sounding horns. The final Hyde Park rally is thought to have involved close to 2 million people, the largest UK antiwar demonstration ever. They were addressed by ex-government minister Mo Mowlam; liberal democrat leader, Charles Kennedy; London's mayor, Ken Livingstone; former Member of Parliament, Tony Benn; the Rev. Jesse Jackson; actress, Vanessa Redgrave; and, among others, the playwright,

Harold Pinter, who described the USA as 'a country run by a bunch of criminal lunatics with Tony Blair as a hired Christian thug'. There were also large rallies in Glasgow and Belfast.

SAN FRANCISCO

On 14 March 2003, 80 protesters from Direct Action to Stop the War (DASW) were arrested in the business district of San Francisco for taking part in a 'direct action' against war in Iraq. Over 200 people assembled at dawn outside the old Pacific Stock Exchange, while some set up a blockade outside the financial trading floor.

At the intersection of Bush and Montgomery Street, about 30 people sat in the street chanting, 'We're blocking Bush!' and were arrested at 8:30 A.M. so that business could continue as usual. On 21 March, more than 1,400 were arrested in San Francisco as protests against the American invasion continued across the city. People chained themselves together at street intersections, rallied in front of city hall, closed the San Francisco Federal Building and blocked the Bay Bridge. More than 100 people were arrested blocking the entrance to the Bechtel Corporation, a major defence contractor, chanting, 'No business as usual, walkouts and refusal'.

INTERNATIONAL COORDINATION

Internationally coordinated demonstrations occurred on 19 March 2003, in San Francisco, Rome, Bombay, Mexico City, Ankara and Halifax, and on 23 March 2003, a quarter million marched in New York.

Again, on 12 April 2003, more than half a million took to the streets of Rome and a similar number in Spain. In Barcelona the protest took a unique form: at 10:00 P.M. every evening, people went out onto their balconies and beat on pots and pans for five minutes. The noise resounded throughout the city, with people on almost half of the balconies in some parts of town, particularly in the old section. There seemed to be few apartment blocks that didn't have a banner protesting against the war, many flying Holtom's symbol. At a protest in central Washington, Dustin Langley, a volunteer with the protest's sponsor, Act Now to Stop War and End Racism (ANSWER), voiced a common perception: 'This is not about liberation, it's about the occupation of Iraq and the plundering of its natural resources.'

HANS BLIX

One of the most respected critics of the war was the chief UN weapons inspector Hans Blix, who

Antiwar demonstrators oppose the impending American-led invasion of Iraq in a March 2003 protest held in Times Square in New York City.

Protesters in Algeria in 2001 sit against a backdrop of antigovernment graffiti, along with a peace sign – 'la pais' – making the point in French.

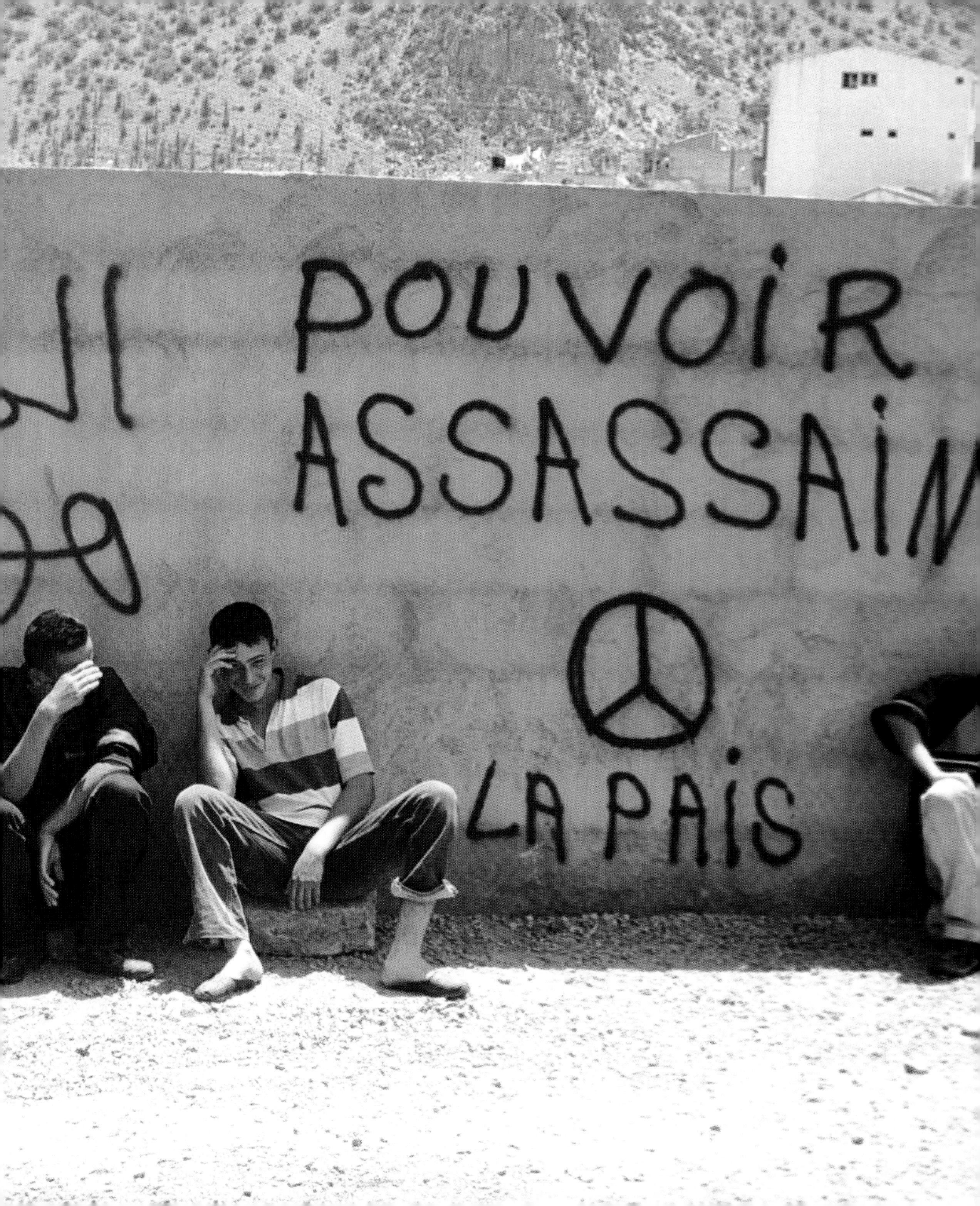
POUVOIR
ASSASSAIN
LA PAIS

'So we must fix our vision not merely on the negative expulsion of war, but upon the positive affirmation of peace.'

— MARTIN LUTHER KING, JR.

concluded that Iraq was invaded for political reasons, not because it had any weapons of mass destruction (WMD). No credible evidence was ever found that Iraq possessed WMDs and it is impossible to believe that Bush and Blair did not know it.

On 9 April 2003, 21 days after the war began, Blix said in an interview with the Spanish daily newspaper *El Pais*: 'There is evidence that this war was planned well in advance. Sometimes this raises doubts about their attitude to the [weapons] inspections. I now believe that finding weapons of mass destruction has been relegated, I would say, to fourth place, which is why the USA and Britain are now waging war on Iraq. Today the main aim is to change the dictatorial regime of Saddam Hussein.'

President Bush, he said, had told him in October 2002 that he supported the efforts by UN inspection teams to verify American and British claims that Iraq was developing biological, chemical, and nuclear weapons. But Blix also said that even back then 'there were people

within the Bush administration who were skeptical and who were working on engineering regime change'.

By early March 2003, Blix added, hawks in both Washington and London had become impatient. It was possible that the USA and Britain did believe Iraq had WMDs, but given the American fabrication of evidence, that belief was doubtful. Amercian allegations, for example, that Iraq had attempted to buy uranium from Niger, were later proved to be false.

'You ask yourself a lot of questions when you see the things they did to try and demonstrate that the Iraqis had nuclear weapons, like the fake contract with Niger', Blix explained, adding, 'I'm very curious to see if they do find any [weapons].'

In any event, none were found and it is extremely unlikely that any had ever existed. Blix said that the war in Iraq was 'a very high price to pay in terms of human lives and the destruction of a country' when any threat of weapons proliferation could have been contained by the UN inspections.

Part of a massive protest in London in 2005, organised by the Stop the War Coalition, against the Anglo-American war policy conducted in Iraq.

'Mankind must put an end to war, or war will put an end to mankind.'

— JOHN F. KENNEDY

◄ A demonstrator holds a peace flag as thousands of protestors converge on Washington during a 2007 demonstration against the Bush administration's proposed 'surge' of troops in Iraq.

A CONTINUING PROTEST

President Bush's ill-timed visit to Britain in November 2003 spurred continuing demonstrations in the UK. The mayor of London, Ken Livingstone, shunned the official celebrations, holding an alternative event honouring antiwar activists, while Bush and his entourage ran the gauntlet of jeering crowds.

In Iraq on 8 April 2004, thousands of Sunni and Shiite Muslims forced their way – nonviolently – through American military roadblocks in order to bring aid from Baghdad to the besieged Sunni rebel bastion of Fallujah, carrying banners and shouting antiwar slogans.

On 20 March 2004, on the anniversary of the American invasion, millions of people took to the streets in protest. In Rome there were more than 300,000 people, and in Heroe's Square, in Budapest, protesters carrying lit torches formed a gigantic peace symbol.

In London a huge statue of President George W. Bush was toppled as part of an antiwar rally in Trafalgar Square – an imitation of toppling the statue of Saddam Hussein in Baghdad.

And on the eve of the Republican National Convention in New York City, 29 August 2004, demonstrators carried 1,000 coffins, draped in American flags, past Madison Square Garden, where the convention was held; each individual coffin represented an American killed in the war. As usual, Holtom's symbol, which had now come to universally represent the idea of peace, was very much in evidence.

Wherever there is tyranny, wherever warmongers are at work, there will be people who will oppose them. And marching with them will be Gerald Holtom's peace sign.

► Protestors unfurled a huge American flag emblazoned with the peace sign on Broadway in New York prior to the 2004 National Republican Convention at Madison Square Garden, in protest at the war in Iraq.

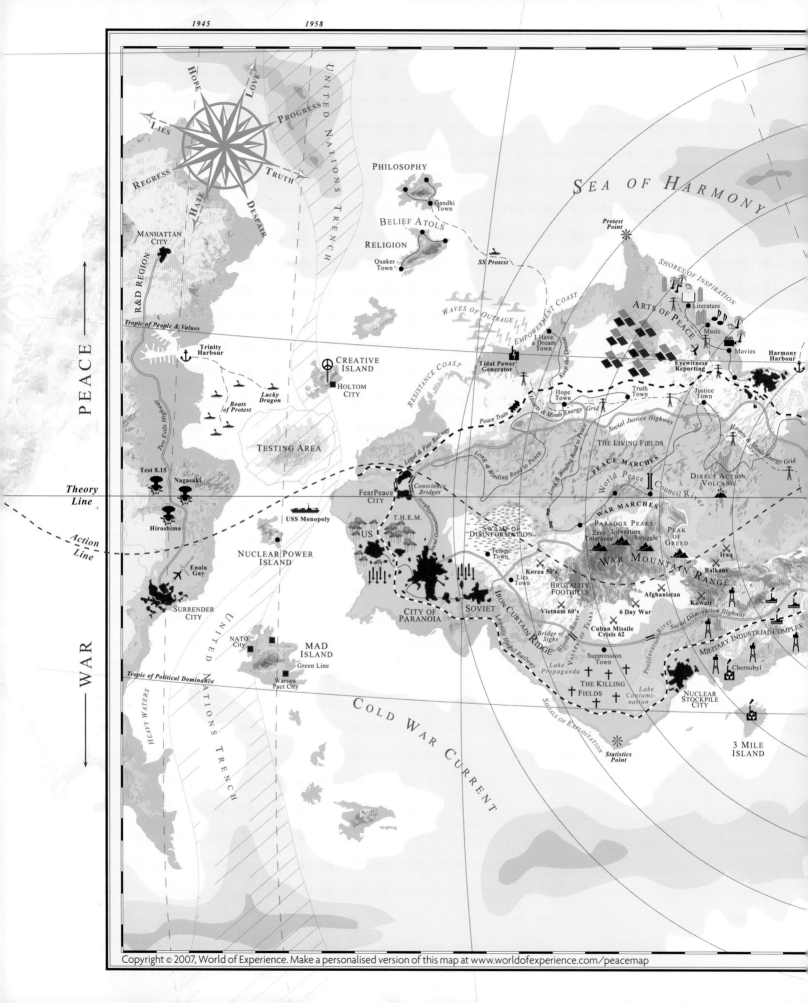

LIES
HOPE
LOVE
REGRESS
TRUTH
HATE
DESPAIR
PROGRESS

UNITED NATIONS TRENCH

SEA OF HARMONY

PHILOSOPHY
Gandhi Town
BELIEF ATOLS
RELIGION
Quaker Town

Protest Point

SHORES OF INSPIRATION

PEACE

MANHATTAN CITY

R&D REGION

Tropic of People & Values

WAVES OF OUTRAGE

EMPOWERMENT COAST

I Have a Dream Town

ARTS OF PEACE
Literature
Music
Movies
Harmony Harbour

Eyewitness Reporting

SS Protest

Tidal Power Generator

RESISTANCE COAST

TRINITY HARBOUR

Two Evils Hill

CREATIVE ISLAND
HOLTOM CITY

Boats of Protest
Lucky Dragon

Hope Town
Truth Town
Justice Town

Keep the Dream

Hearts & Minds Energy Grid

Social Justice Highway

THE LIVING FIELDS

Hearts & Minds Energy Grid

Peace Train

Legal & Fair Railway

Long & Winding Road to Peace

PEACE MARCHES

DIRECT ACTION VOLCANO

TESTING AREA

Theory Line

Test 8.15
Nagasaki

Action Line

Hiroshima

Enola Gay

SURRENDER CITY

FearPeace CITY

Conscience Bridges

T.H.E.M.

US

USS Monopoly

NUCLEAR POWER ISLAND

CITY OF PARANOIA

SOVIET

SWAMP OF DISINFORMATION

Terror Town

Lies Town

Korea 50's

BRUTALITY FOOTHILLS

Vietnam 60's

World Peace Council River

WAR MARCHES

PARADOX PEAKS
Zero Tolerance   Liberation Struggle

PEAK OF GREED

WAR MOUNTAIN RANGE

Afghanistan
6 Day War

Cuban Missile Crisis 62

Iraq

Balkans

Kuwait

Social Domination Highway

MILITARY INDUSTRIAL COMPLEX

WAR

IRON CURTAIN RIDGE

NATO City

MAD ISLAND
Green Line

Warsaw Pact City

Tropic of Political Dominance

Legally Illegal Railway

Bridge of Sighs

Lake Propaganda

Valley of Tears

Suppression Town

THE KILLING FIELDS

Lake Contamination

NUCLEAR STOCKPILE CITY

Chernobyl

3 MILE ISLAND

Proliferation River

SHOALS OF EXPLOITATION

Statistics Point

Heavy Waters

UNITED NATIONS TRENCH

COLD WAR CURRENT

PEACE IN OUR TIME

Goodwill Light

Cape of Goodwill

SEMANTICS TROUGH

TECHNOLOGY COAST

ACTIVE PEACE PENINSULA

RECONCILIATION CHANNEL

Tropic of People & Values

Winding Road to Peace

ACTION ZONE

CITY OF PEACE

Nobel Peace Centre

NUCLEAR WEAPONS-FREE ZONE

Laureate Memorial Park

CND1 (CENTRAL AREA)

THE PROS

Hearts & Minds Energy Grid

Personal Road To Peace

Costa Fashionista

NUCLEAR WEAPONS CONVENTION

Greenham **PEACE CAMP**

David

NO TRIDENT REPLACEMENT

Pax Humana City

WORLD PEACE LAND

Peace Treaty Port

NMD Reef

SS Non-Proliferation

SS CTBT

THE CONS

TECHNOLOGY COAST

DEAFCON

NEOCON

Legally Illegal Railway

USABLE NUKES MOUNTAINS

Highway of No Return

DOOMED STRAITS

CASUALTY BEACH

Tropic of Political Dominance

CONFLICT OCEAN

ESCALATION PENINSULA

WMD Desert

Star Wars

The expression 'roadmap to peace' has been widely used to give the impression that leaders have a plan. In reality the roadmap is most meaningful when you are actually making the journey. Marchers for Peace have known this for some time and many have contributed to the creation of this map. View the peacemap online, make a personalised version or send an eCard at www.happybirthdaypeace.com.

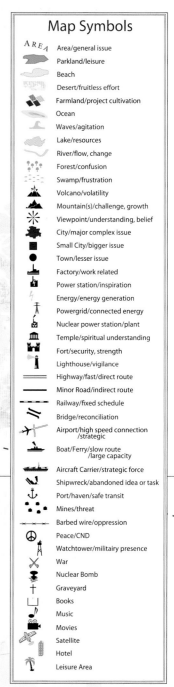

Map Symbols

- Area/general issue
- Parkland/leisure
- Beach
- Desert/fruitless effort
- Farmland/project cultivation
- Ocean
- Waves/agitation
- Lake/resources
- River/flow, change
- Forest/confusion
- Swamp/frustration
- Volcano/volatility
- Mountain(s)/challenge, growth
- Viewpoint/understanding, belief
- City/major complex issue
- Small City/bigger issue
- Town/lesser issue
- Factory/work related
- Power station/inspiration
- Energy/energy generation
- Powergrid/connected energy
- Nuclear power station/plant
- Temple/spiritual understanding
- Fort/security, strength
- Lighthouse/vigilance
- Highway/fast/direct route
- Minor Road/indirect route
- Railway/fixed schedule
- Bridge/reconciliation
- Airport/high speed connection /strategic
- Boat/Ferry/slow route /large capacity
- Aircraft Carrier/strategic force
- Shipwreck/abandoned idea or task
- Port/haven/safe transit
- Mines/threat
- Barbed wire/oppression
- Peace/CND
- Watchtower/military presence
- War
- Nuclear Bomb
- Graveyard
- Books
- Music
- Movies
- Satellite
- Hotel
- Leisure Area

Index